Heavy Petting

My dog taught me how to be a mom, and other tales for pet lovers

REBECCA DUBE

Published by Riverside Publishing

Copyright © 2011 Rebecca Dube

Cover photograph by Jonathan Dube

ISBN: 0615476597

ISBN-13: 978-0615476599

DEDICATION

For Lily Dube

Thank you for your unconditional love,
the many joyful walks and memories
and, most of all,
for teaching me how to be a mom

CONTENTS

PET OBSESSION

PETS ARE PEOPLE, TOO

THERE'S HOPE: INSPIRING STORIES

REBECCA DUBE

MY DOG TAUGHT ME HOW TO BE A MOM

Treating your dog or cat like a baby is not something to brag about. At best, an admission of parental love will get you pitying looks and a quiet corner to yourself at parties; at worst you'll be held up as an example of What Is Wrong With Society Today.

What could be a more perfect example of bourgeois folly, the unspoken assumption goes, than substituting a slobbery, stinky dog for a human infant?

Well, I beg to differ. My dog was my baby; and now that I have an actual baby, I see that my dog prepared me for motherhood far better than any of those *What to Expect* books.

When we adopted Lily the beagle from a rescue group, my husband and I were living the blissful life of DINKs – Double Income, No Kids. It was a sweet set-up: We travelled, went to fancy restaurants, slept late on weekends and kept fragile vases on low shelves.

Then along came Lily. Soon, everything we owned was coated in a fine layer of dog hair. Our schedules shifted to revolve around walks, off-leash parks and vet visits. When we moved to Toronto, we chose our house in the Beaches neighborhood partly because we knew Lily would love Lake Ontario.

Sometimes we longed for the days when we could do dinner, a movie and drinks without worrying about what sort of "surprise" Lily was depositing on our living room floor.

But mostly, we marveled at the joy this sweet, stubborn, goofy dog brought into our lives. When my husband taught her to shake paws, he kvelled like a proud papa. Our hard drive filled up with photos of Lily at the beach, Lily in the woods, Lily sleeping, Lily and her Christmas stocking filled with biscuits.

When our parents hinted about grandchildren, I would say, "But you have Lily!"

Then Lily got sick. That's the problem with dogs: They don't live nearly long enough for us to love them as much as they deserve.

An odd bout of panting led to chest X-rays, which led to a diagnosis of lung cancer – a tumor the size of a soda can in a 30-pound dog. With treatment, the vet told us, she might have a few more months. We walked down to the beach and let her off leash; she raced gleefully to the water's edge, stopping briefly to lick something disgusting that had washed ashore. Paws in the water, she turned to us and wagged her tail as if to say, "Ain't life grand?"

You meet the nicest people in animal hospital waiting rooms. As Lily outlasted the initial prognosis of three months, then went six months, then past a year – with no signs of illness apart from some slowing down we could rationalize away as age-related – her story of survival became an inspiration to other owners with red-rimmed eyes who'd just learned of their pet's cancer.

We swapped information about doctors and treatments, but most of all we enjoyed the company of other people who got it. My waiting-room friends never asked me if it made sense to spend all this time and money on a dog. Of course it made sense. She was our baby.

And then along came a real baby.

Nine months after Lily's diagnosis, I became pregnant with our first child. I read up on how to introduce your dog to your baby, all the while praying that Lily would make it that far.

Some days she seemed full of spunk, just like her old self, and other days she would walk into walls and pee in the hallway with a tired, helpless look in her eyes. Preoccupied as I was with the life growing inside me, I couldn't bear to think about ending the life that was dwindling in front of me.

At night we kept each other company in the living room; I retreated to the couch when I became too uncomfortable in bed, and Lily paced nearby. I'd pet her and try to get her to lie down, but she would just look at me impatiently, as if she had places to go. She would make her rounds, from the stairs, to the fireplace, to the window and back again, as I drifted off to sleep to the sound of her nails clicking on the hardwood floor.

Our son, Elijah, arrived 10 days early, and we brought him home on a Saturday night. All through my pregnancy, I'd hoped for the moment we finally got when we introduced Elijah to Lily, and stroked his tiny baby hand against her soft fur. In my greedy heart I wanted them to have years together, for him to laugh at her wagging tail, for her to wait patiently for scraps beneath his high chair. But that tiny bit of grace would have to be enough. Lily died early Monday morning. I think I heard her whisper to Eli in their brief time together, "They love it when you pee on the couch."

My dog was my baby. She taught me that a slobbery, stinky creature could pee on my shoes, poop everywhere, complicate my life in a million aggravating ways – and at the same time inspire so much love that my heart felt like it would burst with happiness. She taught me and my husband how to go from two to three. She taught us how to be a family.

Now the routines of dog walks and vet visits have given way to diaper changes and pediatricians (whom, embarrassingly, I have referred to as "vets" a couple of times, though thankfully not to their faces).

When Elijah gets old enough to understand, we'll show him the photos of him and Lily, and tell him that for a few days he had the best dog a boy could ever want. In the meantime, when he's fussy at night, I take him out to the living room. The only thing that seems to calm him down is pacing the hardwood floor, from the stairs to the fireplace to the window, around and around again, until he drifts off to sleep.

REBECCA DUBE

• 2 •

I DRESS UP MY DOG FOR HALLOWEEEN

I have a confession to make: I dress up my dog for Halloween.

I'm not necessarily proud of this behavior, though my hard drive is stuffed with photos of Lily the beagle as an angel, a baseball player and a pumpkin. And of course there is her Christmas elf costume.

Responses to our Halloween photos usually split between, "Oh my God, that is the cutest thing ever" and "Oh my God, you need to seek professional help now."

Maybe the naysayers are getting to me, but I do wonder whether it's morally right to costume pets. Am I abusing my authority over this trusting, gentle soul?

If I am, I'm not alone - and Lily's baleful response isn't unique. Browse through online photographs of pet costumes, and you will see a lot of thousand-yard stares.

The dogs have the same look hostages have when they're making videos about how well their captors are treating them ("This sailor outfit is totally comfortable. I repudiate the acts of the Animal Liberation Front"). The cats, meanwhile, are clearly plotting ways to murder their owners in their sleep.

With dogs, though, cuteness is not just a human fetish; it's an evolutionary strategy.

Thousands of years of domestication have rewarded puppy-like features and have shaped dogs to be our loyal companions, amenable to our whims, in exchange for food and shelter.

Maybe their canine ancestors would have thought twice about creeping toward the circle of humans around the fire and begging for food scraps if they knew that, one day, Dora the Explorer outfits would be part of the bargain.

But it's too late to turn back now.

Pet costumes hit the sweet spot of two marketing trends: the increased commercialization of Halloween and the so-far insatiable consumer appetite for pet accessories. As Halloween spending continues to grow, a survey by the American Pet Products Association found that 7 per cent of dog owners copped this year to buying a Halloween getup for their dog, up from 4 per cent in 2004.

Devils, angels, pumpkins and bumblebees are the bestselling costumes at PetSmart stores this year, according to Rashell Cooper, PetSmart's buyer of dog and cat apparel. She made the switch from human-apparel buyer three years ago, and still sounds pleasantly surprised that her job exists.

"Who would have thought it?" she says.

Ms. Cooper has seen festive outfits on cats, dogs, ferrets, guinea pigs, even iguanas.

Basically, if it slows down long enough for us to catch it, we will costume it.

"The way I look at it, pets are part of your family," Ms. Cooper says. And what says "I love you like family" better than forcing your loved one into a cheap polyester Wonder Woman outfit, and then laughing and taking photos to post on the Internet? (That's how my family celebrated every holiday, and I turned out fine.)

Despite the PetSmart fashion expert's seal of approval, I was still haunted by Lily's reproachful stare. Am I a bad "pet parent" (as PetSmart calls us)?

I turned to a more critical authority - Alison Cross, spokeswoman for the Ontario Society for the Prevention of Cruelty to Animals - and confessed my dog-dressing ways.

"As long as it's not causing stress or injury, then it's fine," Ms. Cross said.

So costumes that are too tight, that restrict animals' movements, cover their eyes or ears, stop them from barking, or have dangling pieces that could create a choking hazard - those are out. Note she said nothing about costumes that seem to engender feelings of existential dread, cynicism and a numb acquiescence to the recklessness of authority.

"Go ahead and take the photo," Ms. Cross said, just a touch reluctantly.

Phew. Glad that's settled. Now, if someone could tell me where to find eyeglasses and a Sarah Palin wig to fit a beagle, I will be set.

• 3 •

MY MYSTERIOUS MUTT:
LAB, BEAGLE OR DINGO?

When I first read about DNA testing for dogs, I thought it would be one of those silly news items my husband and I could laugh at together. True, we were crazy about Lily, a rescue dog we guessed was a beagle mix, but surely we weren't the sort of ridiculous people who push their puppies in strollers, take their dogs to yoga, and pay $79.95 to determine the ancestry of their mutts, I thought smugly.

How quickly we become what we mock.

"That is awesome," my husband responded. "We have to do that."

Maybe I should have seen it coming. After all, we often speculated about Lily's mysterious past. A veterinarian discovered her four years ago, wandering along a country road - a friendly, well-trained adult dog with no collar, no tags, no microchip and apparently no one looking for her. How did a dog who clearly lives for human attention - at dog parks, she runs up to people, not other dogs - wind up alone and abandoned? I spun macabre stories about elderly owners dying in isolated farmhouses. Lily's innocent gaze gave away nothing.

"I don't think that's a beagle, honey," my mother said in the pitying tone one might use to explain that the Chihuahua I'd brought back from a Mexican vacation was, in fact, a sewer rat. She guessed Lab.

Now we could know for sure.

Certainly, there are reasons besides idle curiosity to test a dog's DNA. Dog lovers in Connecticut recently tested a shelter dog that looked like a pit bull: They discovered she was a mix of boxer, bull terrier, cocker spaniel and bulldog, which they hope will make her more adoptable. With Ontario's pit bull ban, DNA testing could save some dogs' lives.

We had no such lofty justifications; Lily looks more like a baby harp seal than a pit bull. The hair-covered clothes and beagle-sized Halloween costumes in our closet point toward the "crazy dog people" explanation.

And so I found myself wrestling with Lily, trying to swab her cheek with a thin, bristle-head brush supplied by MMI Genomics. The lab offered tips: "If your pet is active and/or difficult to swab, try collecting the DNA sample while your pet is quietly resting."

Ha. When your dog wakes up to find a long bristle brush inside its mouth, he or she will not be "quietly resting" for long. Lily resisted the DNA collection with the zeal of a privacy advocate, but at last I got a sufficient sample.

Weeks later, the fateful envelope arrived. Sensing the excitement, Lily jumped on her hind legs to sniff the letter.

The big reveal: Mostly beagle, with a trace of cocker spaniel. Vindication!

Has this knowledge transformed Lily's life? Not at all, except for the extra treats she enjoyed as we celebrated the results.

Though we proudly hung the "heritage breed test" certificate by her food bowl, knowing her supposed ancestry hasn't changed much for us, either.

Lily has seen me through an international move and countless personal crises. She's let me cry into her fur, and I've stayed up all night rubbing her tummy when she was sick. The laboratory could have told me she's part dingo, part mutant raccoon, and I'd still love this mutt with all my heart.

Now we have an answer when people ask, "What kind of dog is that?"

But there's only one true reply to that question, no matter what the DNA says: "The best kind."

PARIS JUST ISN'T PARIS
WITHOUT YOUR POOCH

It was a picture-perfect night in Paris. As my husband and I strolled along the Seine, the lights of Notre Dame twinkling on the water, he reached for my hand and I looked into his eyes. He didn't have to say a word - I knew just what was on his mind.

"What do you think Lily is doing right now?"

Yes, in the midst of our once-in-a-lifetime vacation, in possibly the most romantic spot on Earth, we were both thinking about our dog. Not that there's much to wonder about: She basically sleeps and eats. It wasn't like she might be curing cancer or mastering agility courses in our absence. Still, Lily was a topic of conversation from Montmartre to the Eiffel Tower, and everywhere in between.

While I doubt Lily would have appreciated Paris, and while we certainly enjoyed ourselves despite her absence, sometimes a vacation just isn't a vacation without your pet.

The travel industry is starting to understand this, and to realize that pet owners can become loyal, and lucrative, customers. More and more hotels, even nice ones, are accepting pets, and airlines are becoming more pet-friendly as well.

Air Canada recently reversed its policy on animals, which banished them to the cargo hold. It will now allow small cats and dogs (10 kilograms or less) to travel with their owners in the main cabin. Southwest Airlines has begun allowing dogs and cats as carry-ons as well. All for a fee, of course.

What if Fido or Fluffy is too hefty to fit underneath the seat in front of you? A new airline, Pet Airways, now serves animals exclusively: Dogs and cats of any size will travel in the main cabin, in crates, with flight attendants checking on them every 15 minutes. Their humans have to fly separately. But at least owners have the peace of mind of knowing their pets aren't freaking out in the cargo hold.

"Us pet lovers, we're crazy about our pets, so we want a more safe, comfortable way to allow our pets to travel," Pet Airways co-founder Alysa Binder told Fox News.

Cities to be served by Pet Airways include New York, Chicago, Los Angeles, Denver and Washington, and their inaugural flights appear to be entirely booked, proving you can never overestimate the pet-craziness of the American public.

But air travel, even in the best conditions, isn't much fun for pets. A road trip, on the other hand, can be just what the veterinarian ordered. Happily, options for getting out of town with a pet have expanded in recent years to include more than just camping and cheap motels.

Bed-and-breakfasts are usually good bets for pet-friendliness. Silvia Brown has been welcoming dogs of all sizes to Clover Field House, her B&B in Niagara-on-the-Lake, Ont., for about 10 years (her website features photos of happy canine customers). Aside from a couple of inattentive owners who left their dogs in the room all day, she reports few problems.

"Most of the dogs are better behaved than kids," Ms. Brown says.

The Fairmont hotel chain, which owns 21 properties across Canada, has long welcomed pets and is officially phasing out its 10-kilogram weight restriction. Mike Taylor, Fairmont public-relations manager, says the rule wasn't necessary or always enforced - which I appreciated when Lily, who weighs in closer to 15 kilos, and I were guests at the Château Frontenac in Quebec City.

I don't think Lily fully appreciated the grandeur of the Château Frontenac or the charms of Vieux-Québec, though she did seem to enjoy the many outdoor cafés and resulting croissant crumbs. But having her there made the trip more fun for me. And when it comes to experiencing local culture, a pet is the greatest travel companion. My French is horribly rusty, but I know what *chien gentil* means, and so does Lily. We may not have had Paris, but we'll always have Quebec City.

• 5 •

WHEN FURBABIES MEET THE REAL THING

'Just wait - you'll see," is one of those phrases that people love to say to expectant first-time parents.

A relative used it when predicting how our attitude would change toward our dog once we have our baby. "You'll see. She'll just be a dog," said my cousin, who knows we dote on our beagle.

As people wait longer to have kids, pets often assume the role of substitute children - they're our furbabies. But when a real (non-furry, I hope) infant comes along, the demotion to "just a dog" can be rough on Fido. On the mild end, your dog might bark when the baby cries, or pee in the house when the new arrival throws off his regular walk schedule.

But the consequences can be more serious. In July 2009, a Kentucky couple called 911 to report that their newborn baby was missing - only to discover him 10 minutes later in the jaws of their family dog, who'd dragged him from his crib into the backyard. The three-day-old baby was seriously injured but is recovering.

Preventing a terrible accident like that is simple: Never, ever leave a baby unattended with a dog. But beyond common sense, there is a lot you can do to prepare your pooch.

Denise Joyce worked extensively with Hank, her eight-year-old rescue dog, before the birth of her first child. The 80-pound mix of Labrador Retriever and Staffordshire terrier was well-trained but, as Ms. Joyce points out, most dog owners tolerate lapses in manners that are fine around adults but problematic with children. It's okay for a dog to occasionally jump on the sofa, for example, but not when a baby is lying there.

Ms. Joyce worked to reinforce "leave it" and "drop it" commands with Hank, who was protective of his toys. On walks, she trained him not to pull on the leash.

"There's tons you can do with positive reinforcement," Ms. Joyce said. "You want your dog to feel really good about the baby but also keep a respectful distance."

The key, she adds, is to start preparing when you find out you're pregnant.

"You have no idea how your world is going to get rocked. There's no time to dog train once the baby gets home."

Ms. Joyce turned her experiences into a workshop for expectant parents that she teaches at It's a Dog's Life, a doggy daycare and training centre near Toronto's High Park. The training she did with Hank also paid off personally; Hank and Jonah, now nine months, are the best of friends.

"Hank was walking beside him in the stroller today and Jonah was talking to him in his gibberish for 40 minutes," Ms. Joyce said. "It just melts your heart."

One of the best ways to acclimate your dog to an infant's presence is by playing a baby-sounds CD.

Jay Harren of Atlanta produced the Dog Meet Baby disc (http://www.dogmeetbaby.com) after trying the technique out on his own dog, a terrier mix named Jack, before the birth of his daughter, Fiona.

"We heard horror stories of people who had to get rid of their dog because they didn't get along with the baby, and who wants to do that? That's awful," he said.

The first time he played the baby sounds, Mr. Harren said, Jack "went crazy" - barking, racing around the house, growling. But it only took a few days of playing the CD and feeding Jack treats to get the dog used to the wails.

"After a while he would just sit there, and by the time we brought our baby home he was totally fine," Mr. Harren said.

I tested out Dog Meet Baby on my dog Lily, whose temperament generally falls somewhere between mellow and comatose. The "moderate crying" provoked no reaction; track No. 2, "screaming," got a slight nose twitch, but otherwise she seemed undisturbed.

The same could not be said for my husband, who wandered into the living room with a concerned look on his face. "Is that really what it's going to sound like? All the time?" he asked.

I told him not to worry and fed him a treat. "It'll be fine," I said. "Just wait - you'll see."

TRUTH IS STRANGER THAN FICTION

• 6 •

DOG CRAZY, OR JUST PLAIN CRAZY?

Thanks a lot, Joyce Bernann McKinney.

You and your pit-bull-cloning, secret-identity-having, Mormon-missionary-kidnapping ways threaten to undo all the hard work of those of us striving to prove that dog ownership and sanity can coexist.

Ms. McKinney bounded into the public eye in 2008 after she paid a South Korean company $50,000 (U.S.) to clone her beloved dead pit bull, Booger, in the world's first commercial canine cloning.

That's not even the weird part of the story.

The widely circulated photographs of Ms. McKinney ecstatically cuddling one of her five mini-Boogers rang a few bells among people who remembered the case of one Joyce

McKinney, a former beauty queen notorious in Britain for allegedly kidnapping a Mormon missionary, chaining him to a bed in a quaint Devon cottage and forcing him to have sex with her.

That Ms. McKinney jumped bail and fled England in 1978 before standing trial. Now, it seemed, she had resurfaced - for the love of Booger.

Ms. McKinney eventually fessed up to her true identity, though she continues to insist the sex was consensual. (That may explain the mink-lined handcuffs, though not the chloroform.)

She told a British court at the time that the whole kidnapping-rape thing was just a big romantic gesture to win back the object of her affection.

"I love him so much that I would ski naked down Mount Everest with a carnation up my nose if he asked me to," she told a judge.

Now, you would think that if you were an international fugitive from justice, you might lie low and not deliberately put yourself in the eyes of the international press by, say, cloning your dog. However, that sort of common sense generally precludes kidnapping a missionary to be your sexual plaything. Or cloning your dog.

Is the line between crazy about your dog and just plain crazy really so thin? If so, a lot of us have reason to worry.

When the idea of commercial pet cloning first surfaced, I thought it was ridiculous - but a small part of me understood the urge. Our love for our dogs is so strong, and their lives are so short. As the owner of an ailing, 12-year-old beagle, I have the vet bills to prove that pet owners will go to lengths that seem extreme. I've endured eye rolls and smirks from people who don't understand my devotion, much as I'm sure Ms. McKinney did on her cloning crusade.

And that's the scary part. What if my concerned friends are right, and dressing my dog in a pumpkin costume for Halloween is a gateway to madness? Am I a few gourmet dog biscuits away from stocking up on mink-lined handcuffs and lying in wait for the next nice-looking young man who knocks on the door to tell me the good news about Jesus?

Perhaps I'm looking at this all wrong. The best part about being mildly obsessed with your dog these days is that there is almost always someone who is more obsessed, allowing us to protect that tender illusion of normalcy.

Sure, I may costume my dog on special occasions, but I would never put her in a stroller. That would be weird.

In that regard, Ms. McKinney is a godsend. (Or should that be dogsend?) Her shining example allows the rest of us pet-lovers to believe we have kept a firm leash on our sanity. By comparison, even the stroller people look good.

The saddest part is, Ms. McKinney ultimately left Seoul empty-handed. After her secret past was revealed, she fled without her Booger clones. Now, the miracle pups are just another litter of homeless pit bulls.

• 7 •

MOVE OVER, ACE VENTURA

When someone suggested to Deborah Maguire that she call a pet detective to help search for her missing Chihuahua, she thought they were joking.

"I thought, 'Oh my God, that's a movie - that's ridiculous,' " Ms. Maguire recalls.

But desperate for something to do, or at least something to tell her heartbroken children, she spoke with Ronda Fraser, a pet detective in Kitchener.

Ms. Fraser immediately offered to drive to Ottawa. Ms. Maguire thought it was time for a reality check: Lola had disappeared during a massive snowstorm a month earlier. Tiny dog plus 75 centimeters of snow equals …

"The dog is dead," Ms. Maguire said sadly.

"The dog is dead when you give up," Ms. Fraser responded. "So, are you going to give up today?"

Well, no, Ms. Maguire thought, not when you put it that way. Thus inspired, Operation: Find Lola was launched.

Move over, Ace Ventura. Pet detectives have gone from punchline to profession. Okay, they're still a punchline, but for those willing to endure the sniggers, their services are in high demand.

When Ms. Fraser started pet detecting as a hobby - keeping her "day job" with the Ontario Ministry of Agriculture, Food and Rural Affairs - she advertised on only one website and expected to get one or two calls a year. Instead, she's worked on 40 cases, and estimates that 75 per cent of the lost pets were reunited with their owners.

"You have to think like a dog," Ms. Fraser says.

She tracks lost pets with assistance from her dog, Jive, a standard poodle. (Don't laugh - originally bred as a water-retrieval dog, standard poodles are ranked second in canine intelligence, right after border collies.) If they're called within two weeks of a disappearance, when the scent is still fresh, Ms. Fraser will start where the missing pet was last seen. On other cases, such as Lola's, Ms. Fraser consults on the phone, offering advice on how to search animal shelters, where to put up signs and common hiding places for animals.

Perhaps her main role, she says, is simply taking people seriously and encouraging them to keep looking.

"I think people give up too early," she says. "A lot of times it's just giving people hope."

Ms. Fraser doesn't accept money for her services, though she says she may start charging for on-site tracking.

Other pet detectives don't share her reticence, charging anywhere from $100 for a phone consultation to $1,000 a day for tracking - and walking a fine line between serving a needy market and taking advantage of desperate people.

So can anyone with a bit of free time call themselves a Sherlock Bones?

Well, yes. (Although the Sherlock Bones name has been trademarked by a fellow in California, so he might object.) It's buyer beware when it comes to pet PIs.

The two pet detectives currently working in Canada, Ms. Fraser and Vicky Vaughan of Dartmouth, N.S., are both certified as missing animal response technicians by the first pet detective school in North America, Missing Pet Partnership, run by former police detective and K9 trainer Kat Albrecht. Ms. Fraser travelled to California for the 5 ½-day, $625 training course, which covers everything from animal behavior and wildlife tracking to grief counseling, probability theory and identifying animal blood stains.

The training paid off for Lola. The day after Ms. Maguire's family distributed lost-dog flyers designed by Ms. Fraser, they received a phone call from a house about three blocks from the spot where Lola disappeared. The home owners thought there might be a dog hiding under their deck.

Ms. Maguire's husband and children peered into the darkness beneath the deck and called Lola's name. After a few minutes, they saw movement, and Lola emerged - starving and skittish, but miraculously alive. She'd been trapped by the snow, and survived by cuddling up to the foundation.

"Had it not been for the persistence of Ronda, we would never have gotten her back," Ms. Maguire says. "She would have died under that deck."

• 8 •

IS YOUR PET RAPTURE-READY?

A new business promises to care for the pets of people who are transported suddenly to heaven in the Rapture, an event that some evangelical Christians believe will precede the Apocalypse as described in the Book of Revelation. Most Rapture experts say that when the faithful go to Jesus, their pets will stay on Earth with the non-believers.

That's where Bart Centre - pet lover and atheist - comes in. For $110, he and his network of pet rescuers, confirmed atheists all, will go to your house in the event of the Rapture, rescue your dog, cat or other pet, and care for it for the rest of its life or until the end of the world, whichever comes first.

The idea for his business, Eternal Earthbound Pets, began as a joke between friends, but Mr. Centre says he recognized a business opportunity and is now dead serious.

He has signed up more than 100 clients. Mr. Centre, author of a book on atheism called The Atheist Camel Chronicles, thinks the Rapture is bunk - which means the $11,000 he's collected so far is easy money. But he says he's not doing anything unethical by capitalizing on a belief he does not share.

"Lots of people say this is a scam, but I am not promoting the Rapture. I did not come up with Rapture doctrine," says Mr. Centre, 61, a retired retail executive who lives in New Hampshire. "If you believe in it, and you're concerned about your pets, I'm here to help you."

In the six months after his website (eternal-earthbound-pets.com) went live in June 2009, Mr. Centre says he received about 4,000 e-mails.

Most (85 per cent) are from atheists who either think the idea is tremendously funny or want to sign up to be pet rescuers. (So far he has rescuers covering 22 U.S. states; though he's had many atheists contact him from Canada, he hasn't yet expanded here.) About 10 per cent of the e-mails are from Christians, Mr. Centre said; some don't believe in the Rapture and want to compliment him on his amusing business model, and some do believe and are angry with him. About 5 per cent of the e-mails are genuine inquiries.

Terry James, a writer and editor with the popular website RaptureReady.com, says most Christians don't want to think about leaving their pets behind when the Rapture comes. As a cat owner he finds this unfortunate. But he doesn't advise signing up with Mr. Centre.

"I presume he is coming from the perspective [of] a fool and his money is soon parted, and there's a sucker born every minute," Mr. James writes in an e-mail. "I find it hard to invest much confidence in such a business."

But the main problem with Mr. Centre's plan, Mr. James says, is that the Apocalypse is serious business, and he doubts that pet rescue is going to be high on the priority list of anyone who is "left behind."

"With possibly two-thirds of Earth's population prophetically scheduled to die during that last 7 years, because of all of the judgments that God will bring upon a rebellious, unbelieving planet of Earth-dwellers (as the Bible calls them), pets will be among the last matter with which anyone will be concerned," Mr. James says. "People will just be trying to live from moment to moment."

If the Rapture does unfold as Mr. James and other evangelicals believe it will, some animals will be better off than others. In his book The World Without Us, author Alan Weisman imagines what would happen if humans disappeared from the Earth. He describes a city 500 years after its human inhabitants depart: "Long before, the wild predators finished off the last descendants of pet dogs, but a wily population of feral house cats persists."

Perhaps the only thing that Mr. Centre and Mr. James have in common is that they are both animal lovers. Mr. James has several cats and was the proud papa of a beloved bulldog named Buckley who has passed on to that great off-leash park in the sky. (Despite believing that living pets will not be Raptured with their owners, he does believe that pets and their humans may be reunited in Heaven eventually.)

Mr. Centre has two dogs, a Staffordshire terrier named Ella and a pit bull named Maddie, both of whom, he says, are atheists.

• 9 •

OFFICER'S BARK IS A HOWL,
BUT SUSPECTS DON'T BITE

When a shoplifting suspect disappeared into the woods behind Belk department store, police Officer Vinny Bazain knew just what to do.

First he whimpered. Then he woofed. Then, like an eager bloodhound sniffing the air: "Aroooooo! Ar, ar, aroooo!"

The shaking suspect jumped out of a bush, hands up, and surrendered to the police "dog." He looked around and saw Bazain, the barking cop.

"He just wanted to fall flat on his face," Bazain chuckled.

After that, Bazain got a chance to howl his way into America's heart. He appeared on "The Tonight Show with Jay

Leno," sharing the stage with guests Ellen Degeneres and Dennis Rodman.

His Lancaster, S.C., barking bust made him famous, but Bazain, 37, is no pup when it comes to collaring bad guys. He's done the bloodhound impression more times than he can count, and he says it works about 90 percent of the time.

He first imitated a dog as a rookie cop in 1988, when he and his partner in South Florida chased a domestic-assault suspect into an abandoned building. His partner, a veteran officer, said, "Vinny, get your dog!"

Bazain, inspired by previous experience with police dogs, started whimpering. His partner fed him an imaginary biscuit.

"Bark like a dog," he whispered. Bazain let loose with a series of fierce barks and hair-raising howls.

The suspect surrendered, and the cop who barks like a dog was born.

No one paid much mind to his hound-dog act until he came five months ago to Lancaster, population 10,000, and nabbed the shoplifting suspect. Now he's a town hero: People bark at him everywhere he goes, and fellow officers tease him with doggie biscuits in his station mailbox.

Bazain's special bond with the canine world may have started when he ate dog food as a kid to see how it tasted. "Pretty good," he recalls. And he's always been amazed at how police dogs can transform hardened criminals into scared little kittens.

He also dotes on Wandie, a part-terrier, part-pit bull that wandered into his life bleeding and broken on the Miami streets. Every night, Bazain and Wandie howl together and Bazain feeds him cocktail wieners.

Does his mastery of dog language mean he can translate Wandie's howls into English?

"Of course," Bazain says. "My dog would say I'm crazy … and he would tell me he loves me."

If Bazain happens to catch you on the wrong side of the law, don't worry: His bark is worse than his bite.

REBECCA DUBE

PET YA DIDN'T KNOW THIS

• 10 •

CATS VERSUS DOGS: CAN'T THEY JUST GET ALONG

There's hope for peace in our time after all.

Not for humanity, maybe, but perhaps between cats and dogs.

An Israeli zoologist surveyed 200 pet-owning households to determine the secrets of dog-cat cohabitation for a study published in the journal Applied Animal Behavior Science.

The best advice? Start 'em young. According to the study, the keys to interspecies harmony are to adopt a cat before a dog, and to introduce the two animals early in life - younger than six months for kittens, a year for puppies.

"We found that cats and dogs are learning how to talk each other's language. It was a surprise that cats can learn how to talk

'Dog' and vice versa," says Joseph Terkel, a zoology professor at Tel Aviv University.

It's not that cats and dogs hate each other, just that they are hard-wired so differently. Cats are solitary animals; dogs live in packs. Cats respond to startling or scary stimuli by running away; dogs respond to furry running things by chasing them.

In How To Speak Dog, psychologist Stanley Coren describes how dogs and cats use the same body language to communicate different - and sometimes totally opposite - messages. For instance, a dog rolls onto its back to signal submission; a cat uses the same pose to slash prey with its hind claws. A dog with its tail held high and over its back is sending the warning "back off," while the same move is one of the most friendly gestures a cat can make.

So for cats and dogs, being stuck in a house with the other species is like being cornered at a cocktail party by a garrulous bore who is oblivious to your polite attempts to extricate yourself: They just don't get each other's signals.

But Dr. Coren notes that about half of dog owners also have a cat - and presumably some modicum of peace in the house - so clearly the language barrier is not insurmountable.

"Cats and dogs can get along perfectly well, as long as they each have their own territory," Dr. Coren says from Vancouver, where he is a psychology professor at the University of British Columbia.

The Tel Aviv study found that about two-thirds of homes reported a good relationship between their cat and dog. A quarter reported indifference between the species, while 10 percent struggled with aggression and fighting.

One important thing to remember is that interspecies communication is a one-off kind of thing. Just because your terrier tolerates your tabby doesn't mean he won't go berserk if he sees a strange cat streak across his path. Dogs and cats may learn to understand each other's language, but they're far from fluent with the rest of the species.

Experts advise introducing pets to one another slowly, in controlled environments.

Sharon Miko has weathered several such introductions in her full house of three cats and one dog (previously two). As operations director for the Ottawa Humane Society, Ms. Miko understands animal behavior, but mixing species made her realize she had much to learn.

"I did wonder if I made a big mistake at first," she says, recalling the remorse she felt for foisting a boisterous dog on her two cats.

When she asked for advice, her vet suggested getting a second dog.

"Lo and behold, she was totally right," Ms. Miko says. Rudy the terrier entertained Betsy the beagle, and Ms. Miko gave the cats a dog-free retreat by fencing off the second floor. She knew the cats were starting to adjust when she noticed them sitting just out of reach, staring smugly at the dogs below.

Despite the challenges, she says, the experience of sitting on the sofa with a cat on her lap and a dog by her feet makes everything worth it. "Some people are both cat and dog people," she says. "I highly recommend it.

• 11 •

HOW DOMESTICATION HAS
DUMBED DOWN OUR DOGS

If you've ever gazed into the affectionate but vacant eyes of your dog and wondered what's going on inside his furry little head, here's your answer: not much.

At least not compared to his wild counterparts. Recent research has shown that Australian dingoes, a type of wild dog, vastly outperform domestic dogs on problem-solving tasks.

University of South Australia PhD candidate Bradley Smith set up a classic canine brain-teaser: He put food behind a transparent, V-shaped barrier, so his research subjects had to back up and go around the fence to reach their goal.

Previous experiments have shown that dogs are completely befuddled by this challenge. "They usually just fixate their attention to the item they can see," Mr. Smith explained. "They will often get frustrated because they cannot get to it, and will bark, dig, jump. They also will look back at their owners for assistance."

Many dogs can't pass the test within one minute, Mr. Smith said. (After which, one hopes, some kindly researcher takes pity on their simple souls and shows them how to get the food.)

Dingoes are whiz kids by comparison, with most figuring out the task in about 10 seconds. Mr. Smith's research on dingoes, published in the scientific journal Animal Behaviour, shows just how far domestic dogs have fallen in a particular sort of intelligence compared to their wild cousins. And who's to blame for their dumbing down? Us, their doting owners, of course.

"The need for domestic dogs to solve problems has been relaxed because we do everything for them," said Mr. Smith, whose research focuses on animal intelligence in general and dingoes in particular. "They have changed their problem-solving strategies to include humans! By this I mean that when they cannot figure something out, or want something, they seek help from us."

Of course, seeking help from humans involves a different sort of intelligence. While dingoes and wolves have evolved through natural selection to excel at tasks that help them survive in the wild, such as navigating complex environments and finding ways around obstacles, dogs have evolved through unnatural selection

– i.e. breeding – to excel in areas that make them good human companions, such as reading people's facial expressions and gestures.

There are surprisingly few differences between dog breeds (and mutts) when it comes to problem-solving tasks that mimic what dogs would find in the wild, Mr. Smith said. While border collies may be tops at responding to human cues, apparently they're just as ill-suited to life in the wild as golden retrievers and cocker spaniels.

Domestication is the telling factor, not breed, Mr. Smith said.

"I don't ever say that dogs are dumb," Mr. Smith clarified. "Dogs are amazing at understanding and communicating with us. … Sometimes I think dogs are perfect human manipulators and get exactly what they want from us."

Not every species gets dumbed down by domestication. Guinea pigs are one notable exception – a study published in the March issue of the journal Frontiers in Zoology showed that while domestic guinea pigs' brains are 13 per cent smaller than that of their wild counterparts, they performed better at navigating a water maze. Researchers from the University in Munster, Germany, concluded that human intervention and breeding have actually made the little rodents smarter at spatial navigation.

But dogs, it seems, have traded street smarts for social intelligence.

Since humans are responsible for their dogs' lack of problem-solving skills, Mr. Smith suggested we make a bit of an effort to challenge the grey matter they have left.

"I think it is our responsibility to give them opportunities to keep their minds active," he said. "Things like enrichment toys, getting them to earn their food, mixing up feeding times so they are not predictable and letting them interact with other dogs."

So next time your labradoodle gives you a blank stare or your pug gets lost on his way to the backyard, just remember it's not their fault – it's ours. And if you're looking for a smart pet, consider a guinea pig.

• 12 •

VEGAN PETS: WHERE'S THE BEEF?

Vegan pets: It may sound like an oxymoron, but the idea of meatless diets for dogs and cats has been gaining steam recently.

Mainstream veterinarians are generally horrified, but vegans say the proof is in the lactose-free, soy-based organic pudding - in this case their happy, healthy, long-lived dogs and cats.

"People tell me I'm forcing my beliefs on my pets, but that's not how I view it," says Billy, a computer programmer on Prince Edward Island who feeds his dog and one of his two cats a vegan diet. "Our pets are our children, and we have to use the information at our disposal to make the best decisions for them."

Though he says he's a proud vegan, Billy asks that his last name be withheld for fear of being ostracized by his meat-eating neighbours (and, perhaps, their pets). He and his wife went vegan seven years ago; his dog, Riley, soon followed them down the garden path. Riley, an 80-pound Doberman-Greyhound mix, had always suffered from stomach problems, but Billy says switching to vegan dog food (from a Minnesota-based company called Evolution) cleared those issues up.

"He's really excited about eating now," Billy says.

Dogs, of course, are omnivorous. Mine will eat anything, though she's recently taken to backing away from her dry-kibble breakfast, a distraught look on her face, if I fail to sprinkle liver powder on it. Yes, she has me well-trained. Although as a pseudo-vegetarian (no red meat) I wouldn't touch liver myself, I can't imagine depriving her of something that obviously gives her so much joy.

Cats are another story. They're obligate carnivores, which means exactly what it sounds like: They must eat meat. Vegan cat food includes synthetic versions of the meaty nutrients cats need, such as the amino acid taurine (lack of which causes blindness in cats). Billy's kitten, Delilah, has been vegan since she was adopted, and apparently loves her vegan victuals.

"Veganism is about limiting the amount of suffering in the world," Billy explains. "It is an ethical standpoint, but we wouldn't want to jeopardize our pets' health."

He's not the only one balancing ethical concerns with practical matters. Actress Alicia Silverstone claims that her four dogs stopped farting after they went vegan. (Sounds like a good way to reduce the amount of human suffering in the world.)

On a slightly higher plane, the New York Times recently ran an op-ed piece by Paul Greenberg, author of a forthcoming book on the future of fish, who bemoaned the profligate use of wild fish in pet food: About 10 per cent of the global supply of forage fish goes into pet chow, he states.

"Those who feel a vegan cat goes against nature [the American Society for the Prevention of Cruelty to Animals, for one] might rethink a pet's potential footprint before acquiring one," Mr. Greenberg writes. "A carnivore, be it a cat, a dog or a salmon, is a heavy burden for the environment."

Veterinarians are skeptical about vegan diets.

"You really have to be careful," says Danny Joffe, medical director of the Calgary Animal Referral and Emergency Centre. "Every species has their own nutritional idiosyncrasies. The bottom line is, your source for info on your pets' nutrition is your family [animal] doctor, not something you read on the Internet or hear from the person at the pet food store."

Dr. Joffe says some vegan dog foods are nutritionally complete (the brand he recommends is Medi-Cal Royal Canin). But for cats, he hasn't found any vegan chow he considers healthy. Sure, he says, some people may feed their cats vegan diets for years and not encounter any problems. But he compares that to the occasional life-long smoker who never gets sick.

And maybe the desire to make our pets' food cruelty-free indicates a larger issue. "What people don't realize is that their pets are not humans; they are different species," Dr. Joffe says.

Of course, there is an easy, natural solution to the vegan pet-food controversy: Get a hamster. Or a rabbit. Or any of the cuddly herbivore pets available at your local shelter. That way, you can both tuck into a good meal with your conscience as clear as the air at Alicia Silverstone's house.

• 13 •

DIY PET RESCUE:
HOW CPR COULD SAVE YOUR POOCH

Would you give the "kiss of life" to your furry best friend?

An Associated Press poll found that 58 per cent of pet owners say they would try to perform CPR on their animal if needed. Dog owners (63 per cent) were slightly more likely than cat owners (53 per cent) to say they'd go mouth-to-muzzle, and women (65 per cent) were more likely than men (50 per cent).

One person who's 100 per cent behind pet CPR is Matt Armstrong of Toronto. He revived his neighbour's dog, Sheena, when her heart stopped during a walk in the woods. The seven-year-old boxer collapsed suddenly and stopped breathing. Mr. Armstrong checked for a pulse but could find none, so he slapped Sheena on the chest and blew air into her mouth for about two minutes until she started breathing on her own again.

Pet CPR protocol calls for closing a dog's mouth with your hand and breathing into its nose, but Mr. Armstrong didn't know that, so he just took a deep breath and went for it.

"I just stuck my face as far down as it went and started breathing," Mr. Armstrong said. Did he think twice about lip-locking with a slobbery dog's maw? "No, 'cause I love that dog."

Mr. Armstrong saved Sheena's life that day thanks to his animal-lover's instinct. But for those who want to be properly prepared for an emergency, pet CPR classes are now available. Sally Achey teaches pet CPR in Montreal and New York, for instance, and says that while the general public may be squeamish, there are enough hardcore animal lovers out there to keep her classes full.

"I've had people laugh at me and say, 'You're kidding,' and people say, 'Ew, I wouldn't blow into a dog's nose,'" said Ms. Achey, who lives outside of Rutland, Vt. "But the people who come into my class are not at all hesitant about it; they're passionate about animals." Many pet lovers are more concerned about what they might catch from another human than they are about going mouth-to-snout with their dog or cat, she added.

Pet CPR is similar to the human variety, with adjustments for size and anatomy. Technique also varies with breed; resuscitating a Chihuahua is a different trick from breathing life into a Great Dane.

Ms. Achey's own dog, Tucker, acts as a test patient for students learning to take pulses and wrap bandages. They practice rescue-breathing on stuffed dogs. The full-day class costs $129 and also covers other pet first-aid instruction on treating bleeding, choking and broken bones. Ms. Achey has never had to use the techniques she teaches on her own dog, but one student recently reported that she saved her 10-month-old Tibetan Terrier from choking on a piece of rawhide.

"He gulped, it got stuck, and in a matter of seconds he was down," Ms. Achey said. "She was able, without panicking, [to save him.] We place an emphasis on having people be prepared."

According to the American Animal Hospital Association, 25 per cent of pets that end up in emergency veterinary clinics could have been saved if their owners knew and applied just one first-aid technique.

Sheena was lucky. After her collapse, the boxer was diagnosed with a heart condition, and is now on medication and doing well. Mr. Armstrong still walks her daily, along with his two labs. Sheena obviously doesn't understand the details of her resurrection, but Mr. Armstrong says she seems to know he had something to do with it: "When we're walking now, she walks right behind me, staring at me."

• 14 •

CUTE, YUMMY OR GROSS: OUR (IL)LOGIC ABOUT ANIMALS

Why do so many vegetarians go back to eating meat?

Which is worse: cockfighting or factory-farmed chicken? How many laboratory mice should we sacrifice to find a cure for cancer – or baldness? What's the difference between the pests we lay traps for, the pets we pamper and the animals we eat?

Psychology professor Hal Herzog has spent his career plumbing the depths of humanity's frequently twisted relationship with animals and has chronicled his findings in a new book, Some We Love, Some We Hate, Some We Eat: Why it's So Hard to Think Straight About Animals.

It's a fascinating read for anyone who has ever wondered what their dog or cat or boa constrictor was thinking, then wondered if they were crazy for caring so much, especially as they bit into a juicy hamburger. The answer? Yes, maybe a little bit crazy. But that's only human.

Clinging to inconsistent beliefs about animals is part of the human condition, Dr. Herzog writes: "When I first started studying animal-human interactions, I was troubled by the flagrant moral incoherence I have descried in these pages – vegetarians who sheepishly admitted to me they ate meat; cockfighters who proclaimed their love for their roosters; purebred-dog enthusiasts whose desire to improve the breed has created generations of genetically defective animals; hoarders who cause untold suffering to the creatures living in filth they claim to have rescued.

"I have come to believe that these sorts of contradictions are not anomalies or hypocrisies. Rather they are inevitable. And they show we are human."

One of Dr. Herzog's most interesting forays into the world of animal love/hate is his exploration of cockfighting – a blood sport in which two roosters are fitted with sharp metal blades and pitted against one another in a fight to the death, for the amusement and wagering purposes of spectators. Sounds horrible, which is why it's illegal throughout the U.S. and Canada.

Dr. Herzog, who teaches at Western Carolina University in North Carolina, spent time with cockfighters and was struck by their proclamations of love for the animals.

While not won over to the notion of cockfighting as a noble sport, he contrasted the life of a fighting rooster to that of the average broiler chicken. The gamecock gets to run around outside, chase hens, enjoy fresh air, eat a nice diet and generally get pampered for about two years before either killing or being killed in a dirt pen one Saturday night. The future McNugget lives for 42 days without ever seeing sun or sky, often lying in its own excrement, eating processed poultry chow, before being stuffed into a crate and carted to the slaughterhouse.

If you were reincarnated as a chicken, which would you rather be?

And if you agree with Dr. Herzog that you would rather be the gamecock, what does it say about society that cockfighting is illegal while raising broiler chickens is a thriving industry? What does it say about you, every time you chow down on a chicken sandwich? This is the kind of rabbit hole you go down once you start questioning assumptions about animals. (For the record, Dr. Herzog does think cockfighting should remain illegal.)

Dr. Herzog has a way of gently skewering some of the more misty-eyed beliefs we hold about our furry friends. He reviews claims about the benefits of pet ownership, for example. While studies showing that dogs improve human health get lots of media coverage (and I am surely guilty of this), he points out the less-noted studies showing that pets have no effect – or even a detrimental effect – on the owners' health.

In the face of countless inspiring "dog saves owner" stories, he relates the research of psychologist Bill Roberts at the University of Western Ontario, who decided to test what Dr. Herzog calls the "Lassie Get Help" hypothesis. He had owners walk their dog in a park with one other bystander nearby; the owner would then clutch his chest and fall to the ground, feigning unconsciousness. Would their dogs come to their aid, Lassie-style, running to the bystander or barking to attract attention?

No. Not one dog in the experiment so much as whimpered for help. In reality, Timmy would probably still be stuck at the bottom of that well.

Thinking so much about animals is bound to change your habits somehow, and that has been true for Dr. Herzog. He has stopped eating veal, tries to buy humanely raised meat and has cut back on eating flesh in general, he tells me in an e-mail. He has also learned to cut us all some ethical slack: "I have become more tolerant of the ethical inconsistencies I see in myself, my students and in the people around me," he says.

One inconsistency he can't rid himself of concerns his cat, Tilly – even though owning an outdoor cat is tough to reconcile with his love for animals. Domestic cats are estimated to kill upward of a million songbirds annually in North America.

"She is an efficient predator whose greatest pleasure is stalking small mammals and birds," he writes. "I feel guilty for having a serial killer for a companion animal."

REBECCA DUBE

• 15 •

ARE THE DOG WHISPERER'S METHODS SAFE?

The Dog Whisperer, Cesar Millan, has built a media empire on his ability to tame and train the most incorrigible of canines. Millions watch his show on National Geographic each week to see the charismatic star teach hapless owners to cure barking, jumping, aggression and fear in dogs.

But could his forceful methods be ineffective, even dangerous? Some think so. There is a growing backlash against Mr. Millan from dog-behavior experts and dog owners who fear that he could bring punitive training back in vogue, despite long-established evidence that positive, reward-based training works.

"It was a surprise to a lot of dog trainers to suddenly see this very old-style training, and to find that it caught on so quickly," said Stanley Coren, psychology professor at the University of British Columbia and author of several books about dogs, including How Dogs Think: Understanding the Canine Mind and The Intelligence of Dogs.

There's no denying that Mr. Millan and his techniques make great television. Every episode of *The Dog Whisperer* features Mr. Millan swooping into the home of someone with a misbehaving dog, camera crews in tow. He certainly seems to have a magic touch – a few firm "tsch!" sounds and leash tugs from Mr. Millan and the former devil-dogs trot placidly to his side, gazing angelically at their stunned owners. The real entertainment value of the show is watching Mr. Millan teach those owners how to become, in his words, "pack leader," dominant over their own dogs.

"I rehabilitate dogs," Mr. Millan says in the voice-over before every show. "I train humans."

It's the wrong kind of training, critics say, and any rehabilitation may be short-lived once the cameras are gone.

"Practices such as physically confronting aggressive dogs and use of choke collars for fearful dogs are outrageous," said Jean Donaldson, director of the SPCA Academy for Dog Trainers in San Francisco, in a widely disseminated critique of the show. "A profession that has been making steady gains in its professionalism, technical sophistication and humane standards has been greatly set back. ... To co-opt a word like 'whispering' for arcane, violent and technically unsound practice is unconscionable."

Dr. Coren said the methods used by Mr. Millan – who has no formal training in dog psychology or animal behaviour – are a throwback to those used to train German military dogs in the 1940s. "The basic flaw in his technique is relying on the notion that dominance is established by force, and nowadays we know that's not the case."

"The leader of the pack is the one that controls the resources," Dr. Coren said. Thus a well-timed treat to reward good doggy behavior (for example, not freaking out when the doorbell rings) can be more effective than 10 of Mr. Millan's physical "corrections" aimed at curbing bad habits.

The dangerous part of Mr. Millan's methods, critics say, is that they may get a dog to stop growling or lunging, but they won't cure the underlying fear or aggression, thus creating a dog that's more likely to strike without warning.

Respected veterinarian and dog behaviorist Ian Dunbar, who heads Berkeley, Calif.-based Sirius Dog Training, has called this technique "removing the ticker from the time bomb." He and Ms. Donaldson feel so strongly about Mr. Millan's approach that they have produced a DVD titled *Fighting Dominance in a Dog Whispering World.*

(For his part, Mr. Millan has pointed out that his training goes further than the corrections seen on TV that his critics denounce.)

The National Geographic channel runs a "don't try this at home" warning before each episode of The Dog Whisperer. "The telling thing is this disclaimer," Dr. Coren says. "What makes good television doesn't necessarily make good science."

Mr. Millan shrugs off the criticisms, saying his training methods are natural and humane.

"It's the difference between going to school and the dogs being your school," Mr. Millan told a National Geographic interviewer. "One is the intellectual knowledge, the other one is instinctual. I am instinctual."

His pop-culture juggernaut rolls on: In addition to his TV show and DVDs, he has a magazine, bestselling books, a line of dog products and even human clothes for sale.

At a recent pet show in New York, people lined up for three hours to meet him. Jackie Comitino of Long Island, wearing a T-shirt that said "Tsch! Be a pack leader," waited with her two dachshunds, Dylan and Cody. She said Mr. Millan's teachings had changed her life as well as her dogs'.

"Every dog owner should read his books," she said. "I follow his method to a T."

• 16 •

THE NEW LEGAL HOT TOPIC:
CAN YOUR PETS SUE?

'The question is not, 'Can they reason?' " philosopher Jeremy Bentham famously wrote in his 18th-century defense of animal rights, "nor, 'Can they talk?' but, 'Can they suffer?' "

The new question might be: Can they sue?

Animal law classes are the hot new offering at law schools.

Before you reel at the notion of Rover retaining a lawyer to petition for 10 walks a day or the fish suing the cat for harassment, fear not. It's a serious field of study; even in the U.S., where animal law is more developed and lawsuits are much easier to pursue, courts have not been overrun by frivolous Fido filings.

Some experts compare animal law today to environmental law in the 1970s - just emerging from its reputation as a special-interest niche (with a tinge of left-wing loony) to become a solid discipline that is widely accepted and potentially lucrative for practitioners.

Prominent Toronto lawyer Clayton Ruby favors another comparison: "It's much like gay rights were 25 years ago. People sense this is going to be an area of importance in the future."

Lesli Bisgould, a lawyer who focused on animal-rights law for years, teaches the University of Toronto class. "All of a sudden the tide has turned and people are saying, 'This is important,' " Ms. Bisgould says. "Right now is the birth of this concept in Canada - it's really coming to life."

The concept of animal law is almost as broad as that of "people law," encompassing everything from veterinary malpractice and custody cases (when couples split, who gets the pets?) to more philosophical issues of animal rights and personhood.

Many of these issues are hypothetical right now in Canada. Despite recent efforts to change the law, animals are still legally property in Canada, and the courts have been reluctant to humor would-be petitioners who view their pets like furry children.

Toronto-area plaintiff Christopher Warnica spent thousands of dollars in a legal bid for visitation rights with Tuxedo the mutt after he and his girlfriend split in 2004 - all for naught, as a judge threw out his claim, saying, "This case must end here."

But there have been signs of change. In 2006, Ontario courts awarded emotional damages for the loss of a dog; a boarding kennel that lost a dog while its owners were vacationing in Hawaii was ordered to pay the couple $1,417.12 for pain and suffering.

In 2002, the Canadian Supreme Court considered the status of the "OncoMouse" - a mouse that had been genetically engineered to be prone to cancer for research purposes. Researchers applied for a patent, which raised some interesting philosophical questions. Patents are reserved for things that have been invented: So can one claim to have invented an animal? Is a mouse a thing?

The Supreme Court allowed Ms. Bisgould and Mr. Ruby to intervene in the case on behalf of several animal-rights organizations; Ms. Bisgould says just getting a spot at the table was a big deal.

"That was a fundamental moment in the development of animal-rights law in Canada," Ms. Bisgould says. "It was a huge victory just that the court said, 'We agree that the animal-rights perspective is one that has to be heard.' "

(The court rejected the patent application, and later approved a much more limited patent for the luckless rodent.)

Post-breakup battles about who should get the dog or cat may not seem to have much in common with lofty debates about the nature of property and consciousness. But they both speak to the question of how, exactly, courts should treat animals, a question that is far from settled in Canada.

"There's this growing recognition that they're not just like a couch," says Daphne Gilbert, an assistant professor who teaches animal law at the University of Ottawa, offered for the first time in 2007. "Animals are treated as property - we buy them and we own them - and yet family law is starting to talk about them as a special kind of property."

Law students say the uncertainty surrounding animal law is one reason why it is so interesting. There are very few Canadian precedents to study in animal law, which is rather ... well, unprecedented.

"That's the excitement, in that a lot of the decisions haven't really been made yet," says Andrew Brighten, a McGill University law student with a clerkship at the California-based Animal Legal Defense Fund. Though he's never considered himself a pet person, Mr. Brighten says he's drawn by the possibilities of animal law. The field appeals to his idealism, too.

"You can really feel good about what you're working on, and that you might be making a real difference," Mr. Brighten says. "Being a lawyer, I suppose, is inherently about representation, and animals are beings who are unable to represent themselves. ... So I think, as a lawyer, it's one of the best jobs you could have."

PET OBSESSION:
PAMPERING OUR LOVED ONES

• 17 •

THERE ARE CHILDREN STARVING IN AFRICA, BUT I'LL STILL SPOIL MY DOG

The latest sign of the apocalypse: a doggie spa/nightclub, complete with aromatherapy, mud masks, a disco ball and a $300 annual membership fee.

Given its location – in the heart of New York's financial district – perhaps it's a sign that the economy has turned a corner.

Or perhaps not. The market for luxury pet products, by all rights, should have bottomed out a while ago, along with the global economy. Hawkers of jewel-crusted collars and luxury dog shampoo should be crying into their soy lattes. But the pet-products bubble is one that hasn't burst. Our appetite for spending on our furry loved ones seems to be limitless.

At a certain point, it all starts to feel a bit obscene. While people are losing their homes and relying on charity to feed their families, dog owners are paying $45 a day to places like Fetch Club, the aforementioned destination, so their animals can chillax in the lounge area and enjoy a glass of "Barkundy" or "Sauvignon Bark" (both of which are apparently gravy, not wine).

Fetch Club may be an extreme example, but pampering pets isn't just an urban thing, and it's not just for people with too much money and too little sense.

Otherwise rational, level-headed humans are buying organic dog treats and investing in cat scratching posts that could grace the cover of Architectural Digest.

Our culture's current level of pet-craziness makes an easy target for moralizing. Isn't it wrong to spend so much time, energy and money on our pets when there are children starving in Africa, quake victims still homeless in Haiti, and needy people in our own cities and towns?

No.

It's not wrong to spoil our pets because love is not a zero-sum game. We can care about our pets, maybe even too much, and still have compassion for our fellow humans.

While it's true that some people may take refuge in the world of animals as a way to avoid dealing with people – and perhaps they have good reason for doing so – most of us find that loving a pet makes us more engaged in the human world around us, not less.

On a purely financial level, the extra money a pet-lover spends on luxuries is comparable to the $4 latte that so many people purchase to jump-start their days: No, it's not a necessity, and yes, it may be a little silly, but it makes us feel good. Until we all become Mother Teresa and start giving away our worldly possessions to the less fortunate, there will always be a reason to splurge on treats that make us happy – even if those treats are for the dogs.

Of course, it's not all about spending money. All the fancy chew toys don't mean much if we don't take time to pet our dog, cat or ferret. It would be nice if we could remember on our own to slow down and appreciate life, to connect with the ones we love, to simply breathe now and then; but often, we need our animals to remind us.

They remind us how to be human, in the best sense of the word.

Do they need (or deserve) fancy spas or designer duds? Frankly, they don't care. But it's not wrong to show them love, even if it feels silly. So have a laugh at Fetch Club and every newfangled pet-luxury scheme that comes along, then kiss your pet and smile at a stranger. There's enough love to go around.

• 18 •

MEN WHO LOVE CATS ...
AND THE WOMEN WHO LOVE THEM

Any single woman with cats, plural, cringes at that dreaded stereotype - the Crazy Cat Lady.

But there's another beleaguered minority that has been suffering silently in her shadow: men who own, and love, cats.

Dudes with feline friends have historically been put on the defensive. Romping through the park with Rover is one thing, but spend some quality time with Mr. Whiskers and people start whispering about your masculinity.

But recently there have been signs of change. Online, men are professing their love for cats, and congregating with like-minded fanciers. A popular Flickr group has collected more than 600 photos of men cuddling their cats. "Down with rabid dogism!"

cries the group's administrator. (In many of the photos the cat is actually obscuring the man's face - displaying either the residual shame associated with male cat ownership or the feline tendency to hog the camera, I'm not sure which.)

One of the biggest YouTube hits of 2008 was "An Engineer's Guide to Cats," a hilariously deadpan look at the joys of sharing one's life with cats, by engineer Paul Klusman. The video has been viewed more than 3.4 million times, and Mr. Klusman received more than a few marriage proposals as a result. (So far, he's sticking with his cats.)

The new movement is long overdue, says cat lover Michael O'Sullivan, president of the Humane Society of Canada. He and his wife have one cat and one dog now, though in the past they've had as many as four cats. It was Mr. O'Sullivan who introduced his wife, a dog person, to the joys of felinity.

"I like their independent personalities," Mr. O'Sullivan says. As for the stereotypes, he says he knows plenty of macho men who wouldn't hesitate to adopt a cat. "I think I'm fairly masculine, and it's never really mattered to me."

Perhaps the biggest proponents of men who love cats, besides the cats themselves, of course, are women. The Brooklyn blogger behind MenandCats.com says she was inspired by the cuteness of her male friends' love for their cats.

"I love cats and I love men, so I wanted to celebrate that special pairing," says Janice, who asked that her last name be withheld so as to keep her cat-blogging identity separate from her working-life identity. She believes the Internet provides a valuable outlet for proud cat papas.

"Cat owners don't get to go out and show off their cats like dog owners do. Dog owners get to walk down the street and people say 'Oh, cute dog,' " Janice says. "People are proud of their cats and they want to show them off."

And pay attention, single men: Some women just can't resist a man covered in cat hair.

"Cats are creatures of subtle communication," says Dawn Hanson of the Feline Rescue Foundation of Alberta. "The men who appreciate and recognize this quality usually bring a respectful sensitivity to all their relationships."

• 19 •

NEW BREED OF DOG STYLISTS
UNLEASH PETS' FABULOUSNESS

With a few soft words, Jorge Bendersky coaxes Merv, a trembling Brussels Griffon, into position on his grooming table. "It's like dancing a tango," Bendersky explains as he runs his clippers down the little dog's side. "You have to synchronize your heart with the dog's, and just lead him into the positions."

With his celebrity clients, bold tattoos and charming Argentinean accent, Bendersky isn't your average dog groomer. In fact, don't call him a groomer at all — he's a dog stylist, thank you very much. Groomers keep dogs clean; stylists make them fabulous.

"Dogs have become such an important part of our social lives; their style is important," Bendersky says. "If your dog is going to be walking next to your Manolo Blahniks, you want him to be stylish."

Bendersky is one of a new breed of dog groomer — ahem, stylist — who's going way beyond the standard wash-and-clip job. And styling dogs isn't just for the Manolo Blahnik set these days. You can get a fauxhawk for your Yorkie or a dye job on your poodle anywhere from Atlanta to Seattle, including many small towns in between. In Peoria, Ill., for example, fashionista dogs go to GucciPucci, a dog spa, for beautification.

"Two years ago, people weren't coming into grooming salons and saying, 'Can you give my dog a mohawk?' I think it's becoming more mainstream and we're going to see a lot more of it," said pet style expert Dara Foster, founder of PupStyle.com.

Bendersky does everything from variations on the breed standard haircut to more eye-catching dye jobs and creative styles. Prices for a session can range from $85 to $300. It all depends on what the owners, and their dogs, want, he says.

"I will talk to the owner, find out what is the lifestyle of your dog and try to find the haircut that complements that," he says. His clients have included Sean "P. Diddy" Combs, Ellen Barkin and Tatum O'Neal, as well as many "A-listers" whom he declines to name, including Academy Award winners and members of the New York elite.

Often the most difficult part of the job is not the dog, but dealing with the owners. Couples fight in front of him about how to style their dog (his tip to guys: "If you want a dog to look manly, you shouldn't get a poodle"). And celebrity clients call in the middle of the night with grooming emergencies. What sort of emergency warrants a midnight call to the pet stylist?

"Oh, their dog stepped in poop, or pooped on himself a little bit," Bendersky says. And they haven't heard of paper towels? He raises one eyebrow and smiles. "I'll do it, for a price." (That price is $300 an hour for late-night house calls.)

Working at the New York Dog Spa and Hotel in Chelsea, Bendersky says he's seen it all. One client put blush on her dog's face because she thought he looked pale. Another requested henna treatment for her dog because she feared his grey hairs were making her look old — actually, Bendersky adds, that's become a fairly common request. Does he do it? "Oh, yeah."

Beyond Bendersky's New York City clientele, regular dog owners are expanding their grooming horizons by tuning into reality shows like The Animal Planet's "Groomer Has It" and TLC's "Extreme Poodles," which explores the growing world of "creative grooming." Creative groomers use dye, clippers and shears to transform dogs into lions, flowers, dragons, and pretty much anything else they can imagine.

As creative grooming gets more exposure, regular dog owners are asking their groomers for fancy haircuts or a touch of color. Todd Shelly, editor of Groomer to Groomer magazine, says football teams' colors are a popular request.

"It will keep growing, as long as people are educated that it's safe, it's not harmful to the dog, and it doesn't take a long time," says Shelly, who is also vice-president of sales and marketing for Barkleigh Productions, which sponsors creative grooming competitions.

Critics look at pink poodles and cry "abuse." Some creative groomers even get hate mail accusing them of cruelty. But groomers and stylists say that couldn't be further from the truth.

"What is abusive is a person walking into the salon with their dog's hair matted, ears infected, nails ingrown," Bendersky says. "We see that every day, and nobody talks about that. Nobody blogs about that."

What about psychological abuse? Dogs don't embarrass easily, so hot pink ears or a purple mullet don't cause them angst.

"A dog will let you know if they don't want that done to them," Shelly says. "The ones that are good with it, love it. They have that personality, they love the attention and they jump up on that [grooming] table. They certainly don't know that they look like, but they know when they get off that table they're in for a lot of attention."

The trick, Foster says, is making sure your dog is the one who craves attention. Some dogs love being fussed over at the groomer, and others hate it. "Be cautious about doing anything that makes your dog uncomfortable," Foster says. "You have those owners that are just in it for the attention they get. You have to make sure it's the right thing for the animal, and not just to feed their ego."

As for Merv, the Brussels Griffon getting his summer haircut from Bendersky seems to approve of the stylist's methods. At the end of his trim he happily rolls over for a belly rub. "There you go," Bendersky murmurs. "Good dog."

• 20 •

YOU KNOW WHAT YOUR CAT
REALLY NEEDS? A POM-POM TAIL

Every so often a list comes out with the world's most dangerous jobs: Logging, deep-sea fishing, installing power lines, security at Justin Bieber concerts.

Cat grooming hasn't made the list… yet.

It can only be a matter of time. Anyone whose work regularly includes bathing cats should be eligible for hazard pay. Even so, some fearless groomers are not content to let Fluffy go with a wash-and-clip. The new rage in pet beautification is "creative grooming" – using clippers and non-toxic hair dye to create artful designs in the fur of our four-legged friends. Usually practised on dogs, mostly poodles, the art form has recently spread to cats.

"I think it's cute and it's fun," said Danelle German, founder and president of the three-year-old National Cat Groomers Institute of America. "They've been doing that stuff on dogs for a very long time. I thought, 'Why can't I do that on a cat?'"

Why not? An array of sharp claws comes to mind, but Ms. German is unfazed by angry wet cats. She says popular designs for kitties' fur include paw prints, flowers, the classic lion's mane, and seasonal 'dos such as hearts for Valentine's Day.

Joanne Mckenzie of Richmond Hill, Ont., travelled to Ms. German's school in South Carolina to become a certified master feline groomer.

She grooms both dogs and cats, and says demand for creative designs is growing.

Contrary to popular opinion, Ms. Mckenzie says cats are not necessarily self-cleaning. "Cats do not groom themselves, they lick themselves, and in the process they spread all that yucky, sticky saliva all over themselves," she says. "Imagine we did that as a way of cleaning ourselves. How clean would we be?"

Imagine, indeed. Ms. Mckenzie has special cats-only days at her grooming salon. There, cats that don't mind the grooming process might find themselves with a little extra flair – say, coloured pom-poms on their tails. "If they're up for it," Ms. Mckenzie qualifies in an e-mail. "If they're relaxed and calm, and only if!!"

Many cats, as you might suspect, do not find grooming to be a relaxing experience. Ms. German says some breeds take to it better than others – pure-bred Persians, for instance, "are coming from many, many generations of pets used to being handled and pampered by their humans." Another predictor of grooming ease, Ms. German says, is whether a cat has grown up with children and thus has experience being "handled," as the euphemism goes.

Cat groomers insist what they do is not cruel. "We never use any harmful products, never push any pet past what they can handle – that goes for basic grooming or creative grooming," Ms. Mckenzie says.

"We're there to make them feel pampered and loved. They get very excited when their owners come back and make a fuss over how good they look and smell."

Despite these stories of happy cats, feline groomers caution that – much like installing power lines – cat grooming is not something that amateurs should try.

"I don't recommend do-it-yourself cat grooming," Ms. German advises, and she's not just saying that to beef up enrolment at her school.

"You really do need to know what you're doing. I've seen people come in with bite wounds and scratch marks."

• 21 •

IN DOGGY HEAVEN,
NO HUMANS ALLOWED

As summer vacations beckon, devoted pet owners face a dilemma. Leave Fido and Fluffy at a boarding kennel and suffer the big-sad-eyes-of-guilt consequences? Or bring the furkids and spend your holiday picking up their poop and wondering what havoc they're wreaking in the hotel room while you're at dinner?

There's a third option: resorts for pets. The latest and perhaps grandest entry in the market is the Best Friends Pet Care Resort at Disney World in Florida. The 50,000-square-foot complex includes a water park for dogs, a separate "kitty city" and VIP suites with flat-screen televisions – because dog forbid your mutt miss a minute of The Real Housewives of New Jersey.

Not enough? Add extras such as 10 minutes of "cuddle time" for $8, and bedtime stories at $6 a pop (or Hop on Pop, if that's what your pooch wants to hear). Basic boarding rates start at $21 a day for cats and $34 for dogs.

"Pets are family members," explains Deb Bennetts, spokesperson for Best Friends Pet Care, which operates 44 boarding centers in the United States. "They share our lives, our couches, even our beds. It is hard for them to be separated from us – and for us to be separated from them. We want our pets to have all of the comforts of home, and all the attention they are accustomed to receiving."

And if that means paying $3 for tuna on a Ritz cracker for your cat (another extra offered) while you ride Space Mountain, by God it's worth it – to someone.

Pet resorts aren't some crazy new idea. Well, they're not new, at least. One industry pioneer is Ontario's own Lisa Brooks, owner of Happy Tails Pet Resort and Camp, a.k.a. "Muskoka's retreat for the furry elite."

Ms. Brooks has been catering to canine campers since 1996, and launched a cat camp in 2009. For dogs, she offers a full curriculum with activities including water sports, arts and crafts and singalongs (or howlalongs, as the case may be), with dogs grouped according to age, size and temperament. Daily rates range from $35 to $85.

"People still think I'm crazy," she says, but she's living her dream – literally. As a kid she used to lie in bed and dream about being surrounded by dozens of frolicking dogs.

The problem with your average, non-resort kennel, Ms. Brooks says in all earnestness, is "the dog is not treated like a person."

Yet despite the anthropomorphizing inherent in singing Kumbaya to canine campers, Ms. Brooks says she aims to let urban and suburban dogs reclaim their inner doggyness: racing through woods, diving after frogs, rolling in smelly things, on no one's schedule but their own.

In her youth, dogs used to run free through the neighborhood and have all sorts of doggy adventures. "Now, as a good owner, you can't let them out of your sight," she says. "We limit our dogs more than we've done in the past. ... Dogs get to come here and live like they used to do. This is their happy place."

And there's the (belly) rub. Our happy place is with our pets, but could it be that they need an occasional vacation from us and all our weird human stress? Maybe. Ms. Brooks's version of doggy heaven is so alluring that owners ask quite often if they can stay, too.

Nope, her resort is strictly for the dogs. But she does direct anxious owners to a hiking trail that climbs a hill above her property until it comes to a lookout. Some people sit there for hours, she says, just watching their dogs romp through the valley below. Now, that sounds like a pretty good vacation.

• 22 •

PUPPERWARE PARTIES:
THEY'RE THE CATS' MEOW

The 1940s witnessed the rise of Tupperware parties, during which happy housewives discovered the joys of resealable plastic containers. The 1960s saw Mary Kay head into homes. And in the 1970s, Avon exploded in living rooms. Useful? Yes. But one thing was always missing at these sales shindigs: adorable animals.

Finally, we have Pupperware parties.

At these affairs, 10 to 20 pet owners get together, swap tales, have a little wine and listen to a Pupperware "consultant" try to sell them gourmet cat kibble, doggie couture and parrot grooming products. The consultant gets a cut of the sales, the hostess usually gets a product discount and everyone has a good time - except maybe for the pets forced to model their newly purchased clothing.

The two giants of the pet product direct home sales industry are Shure Pets, a Chicago-based company founded in 2002, and Petlane, a Concord, Calif.-based company founded in 2003, both of which have hundreds of sales consultants across the United States. Neither one conducts business in Canada, but entrepreneur and animal-lover Emma Cox has set out to fill that tragic party gap. She started Party Pets in 2008 from her home in Nelson, B.C., and currently has 10 direct sales consultants working for her across the country.

You would think that launching a business right before a global economic collapse would have been a very bad idea. But it turns out that selling organic catnip and rhinestone dog collars is a good bet in a bad economy.

"I would say the industry has been fairly recession-proof," says Britt Beemer, chairman of America's Research Group, a consumer research firm based in Charleston, S.C. "The whole thing is interesting, how people become attached to their pets and what they'll do for them."

To be sure, Pupperware parties (also called Pet Pawties and other pun-tastic names) are more about the indulgent side of pet ownership and less about stocking up on basics (although grooming combs abound). Ms. Cox, for example, sells a "Kate

Spayed" plush squeaky toy (at $11.99, a bargain compared with buying a Kate Spade handbag for yourself).

"We definitely aim for the demographic of higher earners," says Ms. Cox, who specializes in boutique-style items and natural, made-in-Canada products. "Their pets are their children, and they just don't seem worried about spending money on them."

Kari Hlobik, a Shure Pets consultant in Vernon, Conn., reports continued strong sales. "Even though the economy is bad right now, people are spending money on their pets," says Ms. Hlobik, who has been in business since 2005. But she has noticed that people are not buying as many big-tickets items, such as fancy beds (which can go up to $170). More utilitarian fare, such as superabsorbent towels and under-$20 shampoos, are selling well.

But doggie needs aside, home-based sales parties in general hit a sweet spot during an economic downturn, Mr. Beemer says. For one thing, there is a ready supply of people looking for work who will sign up as consultants. And the social aspect plays well, too. You may spend $20 on something frivolous for your pet, but if you get hors d'oeuvre, a few cocktails and an evening of good conversation with friends out of it, then it's not a bad deal.

"It's a cheaper way to go out on the town for a night," Ms. Hlobik explains. "And this is more fun than going to Petco."

PETS ARE PEOPLE, TOO

• 23 •

IS YOUR PET ... PSYCHIC?

Does your dog know when you're coming home? Does your cat know when you're going to die? Does your iguana know whether it's going to rain next Friday?

Is your pet ... psychic?

It may sound like something out of The Twilight Zone – or maybe something out of a parody of The Twilight Zone – but many people are convinced that they do share some sort of telepathic link with their animals. Now, one entrepreneur-turned-amateur scientist is recruiting participants for an experiment to test whether dogs can tell when their owners are coming home.

The trials organized by Alex Tsakiris, the California-based host of the Skeptico podcast, are pretty simple. Participants set up a webcam pointed at the place where their dog "waits" for them to come home – in front of the door, for example, or in the hallway leading to the garage. The owners then leave the house for random periods of time. Reviewing the webcam footage later, Mr. Tsakiris computes how much time the dog spent overall in the waiting place during the owner's absence, and how much time it spent there during the "return time" – the 20 minutes or so before the person arrived home.

Obviously, it's important to vary the return times. A dog that knows its owner comes home at 6:05 p.m. every day may be smart, but not psychic.

Mr. Tsakiris's experiment (more information can be found at www.dogsthatknow.com) builds on the research of Rupert Sheldrake, a British biologist who opened himself up to quite a bit of professional scorn when he published scientific papers detailing his observations of possibly telepathic dogs.

In one experiment involving more than 100 randomly timed observations, a dog named Jaytee waited at the window 4 per cent of the time during the main period of his owner's absence and 55 per cent of the time when she was returning.

Cats have displayed their own uncanny abilities. In 2007, a cat named Oscar adopted by a Providence, R.I., nursing home's advanced-dementia unit made headlines when it was revealed he seemed to know when a patient was about to die.

In more than 25 cases, the generally aloof Oscar snuggled up to residents who then died within a few hours, even though many of them appeared perfectly fine at first. Doctors said they believed there must be some sort of biochemical explanation – they just didn't know what it was.

So if this phenomenon is well known, why do more experiments? Because, Mr. Tsakiris says, he wants to wear down the skeptics with more data.

"There is incredible resistance to this. People who say these kind of things are really attacked pretty viciously," Mr. Tsakiris says. "There's a lot of very good, competent research out there that seems to get suppressed or, even worse, derided because it doesn't conform to the whole atheistic materialistic paradigm that dominates science."

In general, I have to say the whole atheistic materialistic paradigm that dominates science works pretty well for me. Claims of psychic abilities rightly arouse suspicion, especially when they are so often accompanied by sales pitches.

And yet, Mr. Tsakiris is onto something in that if you want to find a hardened skeptic's gooey, open-minded center, his dog is probably a good place to start.

"There's this thing called love, and when we love something it creates this real, measurable bond, and it links us up to other beings," Mr. Tsakiris says.

Deborah Beaven of Toronto is so used to living with telepathically in-tune dogs that she was surprised anyone even needed to research it. She says her Great Dane, Journey, consistently waits for her by the window for 10 minutes before she arrives home. Ms. Beaven doesn't work regular hours, so she comes home at different times each day, and the window doesn't even overlook the front of her apartment building, so it's not as if Journey can hear her car, or see or smell her coming. And yet her son has discovered that when the dog goes to the door, she doesn't want to go for a walk – she's just waiting for Deborah.

Ms. Beaven says she was going to participate in Mr. Tsakiris's experiment, but her mother became ill and she didn't have the time to devote to randomized trials. Still, she has little doubt about what it will find.

"I think dogs are as in tune with us as we allow. If we're open, they're right there," Ms. Beaven says. "They're just pure souls, so I think their psychic abilities come out a lot clearer and easier."

It's easy to scoff at talk of pure souls and psychic abilities, but anyone who's ever looked into their dog's eyes with love, and seen that love reflected back, may well wonder what else lies beneath the surface.

A deep telepathic bond? Or are they just wondering whether you have any liver treats? Maybe one day we'll find out.

• 24 •

LADY GAGA, DOGGIE-STYLE

A San Francisco photographer is taking the pop provocateur Lady Gaga's dramatic fashion statements to new heights of absurdity with the Doggie Gaga Project, in which he photographs dogs dressed in outlandish Gaga-inspired outfits.

Picture a pit bull wearing a disco-ball mask and strapless dress, a Boston terrier sporting a lacy red gown and a hat as tall as he is, and another pit bull wearing an outfit made entirely of Kermit the Frog dolls.

Like Lady Gaga herself, the Doggie Gaga Project blurs the lines between madness, creative genius and hilarity.

Jesse Freidin, who makes his living as a dog photographer, stumbled into this sideline through his interest in classic Polaroid film. When the company decided to revive its instant camera business last year and named Lady Gaga as "creative director," Mr. Freidin joked on Twitter about combining all his passions – dogs, Polaroids and Gaga. Then the joke turned serious.

jesse freidin . photographer

With help from The Impossible Project, a group based in the Netherlands dedicated to producing film for instant Polaroid cameras, the Doggie Gaga project was born.

It takes a special sort of dog - a very, very patient sort of dog - to be Gaga material. The five pets featured in the project include Mr. Freidin's Boston terrier, Pancake, and friends' dogs that he knew would enjoy, or at least tolerate, being dressed up and photographed.

The outfits are made with help from artist friends and cheap supplies from a craft store.

jesse freidin . photographer

"We chose the outfits we wanted to do and tailored them to the dogs we thought would do best with them," Mr. Freidin explained. For example, Pancake's tall, red hat expresses the big personality inside the little dog, while Gunther the pit bull was able to get in touch with his inner diva by sporting Gaga's disco-ball getup.

"All the dogs had fun," Mr. Freidin said. "And we gave them tons of treats."

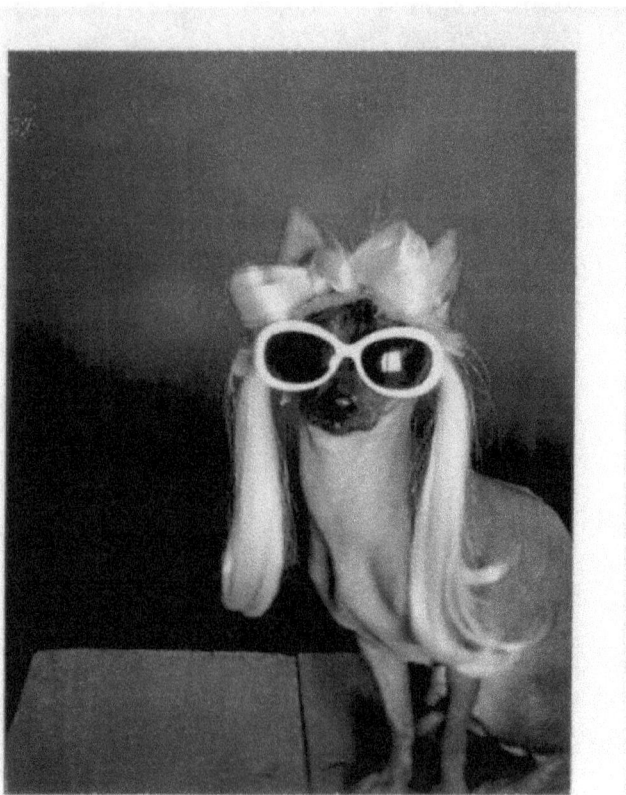

jesse freidin . photographer

Mr. Freidin hoped that the project might bring some attention to what he believes are the underappreciated wonders of Polaroid film. The reaction was much larger. The Doggie Gaga project has been featured on Perez Hilton.com, Live! With Regis and Kelly, MTV and MuchMusic. Apparently, dogs dressed up as pop stars is an idea that strikes a chord with a lot of people.

Due to popular demand, Mr. Freidin has shot round 2 of the Doggie Gaga project, and is working on a book. The fruits of his labors, as well as any Doggie Gaga updates, can be found on his Facebook page, http://www.facebook.com/pages/The-Doggie-Gaga-Project/365443474450.

Photographing dogs isn't much different than taking pictures of people, says Mr. Freidin, who has been working with pooches full-time for about five years. In both cases, he wants to capture an emotional truth about the subject's personality – although with dogs, the process might involve romping on the floor.

"With dogs, I want to know who they are. I want to roll around on the ground with them and become part of their world," Mr. Freidin explained. "I always say to people, the best images are the ones that you really get when you're not thinking too hard about it, just letting the energy guide your images."

And if the energy you want to capture is Canine Lady Gaga? Well then, just dance.

• 25 •

THESE ANIMALS HAVE MORE FACEBOOK FRIENDS THAN YOU

I'll admit I was late to the social networking party. Once I joined Facebook, though, I soon realized it was a wonderful way to reconnect with friends and find out which of the mean girls from high school had gotten really fat.

One thing I didn't count on, however, was that Facebook would return me to high school in other ways – like my creeping insecurity about the number of friends I have. I know it's not cool to care, but I can't help but notice when others have lots more Facebook friends than me. Especially when those others are covered in fur and lack opposable thumbs for writing clever status updates.

Which leads me to this list, which is a handy guide to the world of animals on Facebook and not at all a poorly veiled cry for more virtual friends. (NB: Yes, Facebook nerds, I know these are technically fan pages, and I'm equating fans to friends here. The point: Why do more people like these guys than me?)

1. Paul the psychic octopus: 71,943 friends. A resident of the Sea Life aquarium in Oberhausen, Germany, Paul the Octopus correctly predicted the winners of eight World Cup matches. Before each match, Paul was presented with two boxes, each containing a mussel and marked with the flag of one of the national teams, culminating in his correct prediction of Spain over the Netherlands in the final. Having refused, going through his trainers, offers to relocate to Spain, Paul retired from the soccer psychic business, and seems to be mainly posting music videos these days. He is a Renaissance cephalopod.

2. Oscar the death-predicting cat: 2,302 friends. Oscar is the nursing-home cat that showed an uncanny knack for knowing which elderly resident was next to die. As detailed in an article in the New England Journal of Medicine, and then in a book called *Making Rounds with Oscar*, the cat would curl up next to certain patients who, more often than not, would die soon after. (For suspicious minds, no, the cat was not actually killing the patients.) Oscar favours quotations from Elizabeth Kubler-Ross. As psychic friends go, I'd rather hang out with Paul.

3. Animal, from the Muppets: 77,815 friends. Can't really argue with this. Animal is awesome. In his member profile, Animal identifies his genre as "BEAT DRUMS! BEAT DRUMS!" Classic Animal.

4. Riot Dog: 33,714 friends. This Athens stray has attended every major protest since 2008, and he's in the news photos to prove it. He follows in the paw prints of another Athens protest regular, Kanellos, who by most accounts passed away in 2008 (and yet still has 2,412 Facebook friends. To recap: a dead, homeless dog has more friends than I do.) One commenter on Riot Dog's Facebook page muses, "Does he believe in the overthrow of private ownership? Does he see the rioters as his pack? Does he just hope that the police are going to start throwing those big sticks for him to fetch?" We can only wait for Riot Dog's eventual autobiography to answer these questions.

5. Mystery Monkey of Tampa Bay: 80,729 friends. This rhesus macaque on the lam has been outwitting trappers and shrugging off tranquilizer darts in the Tampa Bay area and has garnered quite the following for his freedom-loving ways. His occasional spottings and imagined inner life are chronicled on his Facebook page, which lists personal interests including bananas, swinging through trees, the theory of relativity and postmodern art.

6. Christian the Lion: 21,230 friends. In swinging 1969 London, two friends purchased a lion cub from Harrods department store and raised him until he was a year old. Then,

realizing that a London apartment was not such a great place for a lion, they handed him over to a wildlife conservationist in Kenya to rehabilitate Christian back into the wild. A year later, the two men travelled to Kenya to try to find Christian – and you've got to watch the YouTube video to see what happens next, complete with cheesy Whitney Houston soundtrack. Don't mind me, I'll just be over here tending to something in my eye … uh, allergies. Sniff.

7. Sparkles the Fire Safety Dog: 2,666 friends. Come on. Christian the Lion I can understand, but this is just embarrassing. This Dalmatian with a kind of lame name has more friends than I do? And consider this recent status update: "Almost 2,700 friends. Woo hoo!" Way to rub it in, fire safety dog. Okay, he does look pretty cute in his red firefighter's hat. Still, I have to take issue when he says that a fire alarm "is telling you GET OUT! GET OUT!" Sometimes in my house it's just telling you that dinner is READY! READY! So, easy there, Sparkles.

8. Max the Wiener Dog: 136 friends. At last! An animal with exactly the same number of Facebook friends as me. Max is a soulful black-and-tan dachshund who seems to reside in Wisconsin, and according to his profile he enjoys "snuggling, taking naps in the sun [and] burrowing under blankets." Me too! What I appreciate about Max is that unlike some other Facebook animals (coughcoughRiotDogandMysteryMonkey), Max does not weigh in on politics or current affairs, but sticks to doggish

observations about tummy rubs and the simple pleasures of rolling in freshly cut grass. Don't ever change, Max – especially not your friends list.

• 26 •

PSYCHO KITTY, QU'EST-CE QUE C'EST?

You can't flick through your cable channels these days without landing on a show dedicated to disobedient dogs. If Rover barks too much or Spot bites the hand that feeds him, chances are you can find answers in any number of TV programs, books and even movies.

But really, dogs? Are they that hard to figure out? Feed them, pet them, throw them a Frisbee, call it a day.

Cats, on the other hand - now there's a challenge. "Dog Whisperer" Cesar Millan can soothe a pack of snarling Rottweilers in seconds, but I have a feeling one bitter house cat could break him like a dry Milk-Bone.

Few experts go where dog trainers fear to tread. But cat psychology is a real field that fills a need for desperate owners.

And feline behavior experts know the stakes are high: Cats are the most popular domestic pet in North America, and behavior issues are the No. 1 reason owners surrender kitties to humane societies and animal pounds.

Carole Wilbourn, a New York-based cat therapist, has been working on feline problems since the 1970s. The issues have remained basically the same, she says: aggression, timidity, destructive tendencies and not using the litter box are top complaints. What has changed are owners' attitudes. They're more likely to seek her out pro-actively - getting advice before moving with a cat, or introducing another pet into the household. And they're less embarrassed about seeing a cat shrink.

"People still have a hard time calling me, but it used to be harder before," Ms. Wilbourn says.

Cats can be more challenging therapy patients than dogs, she says. "Because a dog wants so much to please. A cat is, like, 'Maybe. If I'm happy, then you're happy.' "

From an evolutionary standpoint, this makes sense. Humans have shaped the evolution of dogs more than any other species. Even when they misbehave, dogs are hardwired to please people. Cats, not so much.

But it's a mistake to think that cats don't care, says Pearl Kam, founder of Gentlecare Natural Pet Products in Port Coquitlam, B.C.

As part of her holistic treatment of cats, dogs and horses, she often uncovers emotional issues beneath the physical problems, she says: especially in felines.

"Most people think dogs are the social animals; but cats, when they live with you, they want to be with you," Ms. Kam says. "They do need that bond."

Difficulties often start when the owner takes a vacation or starts working longer hours, she says. "When they get ignored, and they don't get their hugs and kisses, yeah, they get pissed off."

And cats are quick to anger, Ms. Kam says. "Cats won't take as much crap before they get behavior issues. Dogs can have a lot of damage before they show you anything. Cats will show you early on."

But frustrated owners looking to lay blame should take a long, hard look in the mirror, says cat behaviorist Mieshelle Nagelschneider of Seattle. "The majority of feline behavior issues are not true 'behavior problems,' " says the author of Through the Eyes of a Cat, due out in 2011. "They're part of a cat's natural behavior repertoire. It's the owners who have issues with how their cat is naturally reacting to the environment the owner has set up."

Issues often go unsolved, Ms. Kam says, because most cats live indoors, unlike dogs. If your pooch lunges like a maniac when you take it on walks, that's an issue of public safety that must be dealt with. House cats don't present such concerns (even though urine sprayed on a new couch may seem like a matter of life and death).

So will naughty cats ever get their moment in the media spotlight? Not likely. Ms. Wilbourn points out that dog misbehavior tends to be more telegenic: barking, jumping and running in circles makes for better TV than a cat glowering under the bed, silently plotting its revenge for your late work nights.

Even for the experts it takes longer than half an hour, minus commercial breaks, to unravel the mysteries of the feline mind.

• 27 •

NEW DOG SCIENCE
COULD HELP HUMANS

Beth Daly always believed that owning dogs made her life better. After all, she grew up with dogs, she met her husband while walking her pooch in the park, and she enjoys doing animal therapy work with her yellow Labrador at a hospital in Windsor, Ont.

But it wasn't until the elementary-school teacher went back to university to earn her PhD that she realized that relishing the human-animal bond could be more than a hobby - it could be her calling.

"Sometimes I can't believe I get to study this," says Dr. Daly, now an associate professor at the University of Windsor. "It is a lot of fun."

A lot of fun - but also a growing field of serious study. When the Research Center for Human-Animal Interaction held its first annual conference in 2009 in Kansas City, Mo., in conjunction with the International Society for Anthrozoology, a handful of Canadian academics presented research on topics including perception of breed friendliness, the link between animal abuse and empathy development, dog-assisted reading programs for children, and attitudes toward service dogs for the deaf.

Unfortunately, a lot of the research in the emerging human-animal interaction field is afflicted with the "duh" factor: the hypotheses and conclusions seem obvious. But when the answers are surprising, they can have important applications.

Dr. Daly, who studies empathy in children and adults, has found a consistent link between dog ownership and greater empathy. People with dogs, she said, have "a heightened ability to spontaneously employ skills that relate intuitively to social understanding." (She's found no such link between cats and empathy.)

While those insights may not be shocking, at the conference she presented research on the effects of animal abuse on humans. Interestingly, she found that people who have witnessed animal abuse score high on measures of "cognitive empathy" - understanding someone else's pain - while registering low on "emotional empathy" - feeling another's pain.

Her findings, which she is attempting to replicate in a larger study, could have implications for animal-shelter workers and others who deal with violence and abuse. Similar research is raising questions about whether veterinarians should be mandated to report suspicions of animal abuse to human social-service agencies because there's such a strong correlation between harm to animals and child and spousal abuse.

On the lighter side, but no less intriguing, researchers at the University of Alberta studied which dog breed would make the best "social lubricant" between strangers. They compared reactions to a Doberman pinscher, miniature pinscher, Bernese mountain dog and King Charles cavalier spaniel (all breeds with similar color markings). You'd think the small, doe-eyed spaniel would be the obvious choice, but that wasn't it, the researchers say. (They're saving their results for publication, but my money is on the big, shaggy Bernese mountain dog.)

"We hypothesized the small dogs would be much more popular, but they surprised us," says Alicia Glasier, a University of Calgary undergraduate who worked on the study. Asked about the practical value of the results, the researchers point to their finding that a better understanding of various breeds also increased social trust between strangers.

And, of course, there is the fact that one person's "social trust" is another's "babe magnet." Research into the most socially lubricating breeds would certainly be of keen interest to single people at dog parks.

The pet industry in Canada is a market estimated to be worth about $4-billion a year, so it's only reasonable to study what benefits, if any, society is getting from our investment in furry friends. When you read the research about pets contributing to empathy in children, lowering blood pressure in adults and decreasing loneliness in the elderly, it's easier to put up with a little dog hair on the sofa.

One question that researchers don't seem to be asking, though, is whether the benefits of animal-human interaction go both ways. Do puppies develop better empathy when they're exposed to children? Does frequent walking by overweight, middle-aged people reduce the chance of heart disease in adult dogs?

We assume that our pets are better off with us - and thousands of shelter animals would agree - but isn't that a hypothesis worth testing? Doctoral candidates, your dissertation awaits.

THERE'S HOPE:
INSPIRING STORIES

• 28 •

SOLDIERS HELP CANINE REFUGEES

The four-week-old puppy stumbled into the Canadian soldiers' mess tent in Afghanistan, orphaned and malnourished.

The soldiers took pity on the tiny refugee and fed him their rations, which he gobbled so quickly that his stomach bloated, earning him the name "Guts."

In short order the dog became the mascot of the remote outpost, greeting the soldiers when they returned from patrols and curling up on one of their cots every night.

But soon it was time for the troops to move on, and if Afghanistan is a tough place for people, it's even bleaker for puppies. Dogs are generally used for protection or for fighting. Rabies and distemper run rampant, and stray dogs are commonly shot – the fate that befell Guts's mother and litter-mates.

The soldier's credo kicked in: Leave no man behind.

"They were putting dogs down at most of the camps. We couldn't let that happen and he was too small to fend for himself in the wild," writes Private Geordon Roy-Hampton in an e-mail from Afghanistan.

Pte. Roy-Hampton, who had formed a strong bond with Guts, recalled hearing a rumor that there are ways to get dogs out of Afghanistan – for a price. After dozens of e-mails, he connected with Nowzad Dogs (www.nowzaddogs.co.uk), an organization dedicated to bringing soldiers' dogs – and the occasional cat – home from Afghanistan and Iraq. With its help, Guts was transported to Kabul.

As Guts made the perilous journey, friends of Nowzad Dogs and Pte. Roy-Hampton raised the roughly $3,000 needed to get him to Canada. And in April 2010, the spindly white-and-tan puppy bounded out of his crate at Toronto's Pearson airport and into the arms of Sandra Roy, Pte. Roy-Hampton's aunt.

Guts isn't the only canine Afghan refugee to find a new home in Canada. Though Canadian Forces official policy forbids camp pets, stray dogs and lonely soldiers have a way of adopting one another.

Corporal Samantha Parsons befriended a large, fluffy white dog named Delilah while stationed in Afghanistan. She decided to bring the canine home after her best (human) friend was injured and returned to Canada.

"That's when I really bonded with her," Cpl. Parsons explains in an e-mail. "She's basically my very, very expensive mental-health plan and she was more than worth every penny."

Delilah made the trip to Newfoundland from Islamabad, where she's staying with Cpl. Parson's grandmother until the soldier's tour of duty ends.

None of these dogs would ever escape Afghanistan without the efforts of dozens of dedicated volunteers, some of whom put themselves at great personal risk. The Taliban are not keen on locals aiding Coalition forces, and that includes helping their dogs.

Penn Farthing, the retired British soldier who runs Nowzad Dogs, got involved in animal rescue when he broke up a dog fight outside his compound soon after arriving in Helmand Province in 2006. One of the fighting dogs attached himself to him, and one stray soon led to another, and another. One morning he woke up to seven new arrivals: A mama dog had crept under the gate in the middle of the night and then carried her six puppies into the compound, one by one.

It wasn't the mission he'd signed up for, but Mr. Farthing couldn't resist those puppy eyes.

"It felt really good to actually be doing something positive, even if it was by looking after some mangy strays," Mr. Farthing said. "The Taliban did a real good job of disrupting our reconstruction efforts for the local people, so looking after the dogs gave us a few minutes of respite each day, and the dogs were always happy to see us."

On the Canadian end of the journey, another retired military man is helping out. Albert Wong, retired after 32 years of service in the Canadian Forces, helped facilitate the arrival of Guts and Delilah in Toronto, shepherding them through health inspections and customs.

"You're facing very difficult choices, and a dog gives you unconditional love," Mr. Wong explained. "For me, doing this is a small way to help the soldier in the field."

As for Guts, he's been renamed Gus and is living the good life on a Regina farm owned by Pte. Roy-Hampton's mother. When he first came out of his crate, he licked Ms. Roy's face, took some water from her husband, then began sniffing his new surroundings. "He seemed alert, but not wary," Ms. Roy said. "Almost as though he was looking for someone who wasn't there."

Pte. Roy-Hampton's family is counting the days until his return. Until then, they've got Guts.

• 29 •

TOUGH GUYS, TENDER HEARTS

You won't find any Birkenstock-wearing, hybrid-driving, gentle souls at Rescue Ink. The eight large men who make up the animal rescue group favor steel-toed boots, Harley-Davidsons and bad attitudes; the name is a play on their heavily tattooed bodies. They respond to reports of animal abuse and neglect in force, literally flexing their muscles and pouring on the intimidation to confront suspected cat shooters, bird poisoners and dog beaters.

"Our approach is different than other rescue groups," acknowledges Joe Panz, a founding member of Rescue Ink who, like the other members, prefers to go by his nickname (his full moniker is Joseph Panzarella). "If we find a person abusing an animal, we 'educate' him our way. Quite frankly, we can be very persuasive."

Can't you just hear the testosterone? The men's dramatic appeal caught the eye of reality-TV producers, and now the tough-guy stylings of the group can be seen on Rescue Ink every Tuesday night on cable television (on TVtropolis).

Mr. Panz says the group (rescueink.org) started simply as a gathering of friends, motorcycle enthusiasts who grew up together and shared a soft spot for animals. They organized formally after confronting a man who had set his dog on fire. What happened?

"I'd rather not say," Mr. Panz replies in his New York-accented rasp. "We drove our point home, let's just say."

Note: This was before they had cameras in tow.

On the show, Mr. Panz and the other Rescue Ink members confront suspected animal abusers in the greater New York area with icy stares, crossed arms (the better to show off those tattooed biceps), raised voices and the impression of barely constrained violence.

"You don't send a Boy Scout after a bad guy, you fight fire with fire," says Mr. Panz, whose background includes being shot five times for reasons he cares not to discuss. That incident set him on the straight, if not the narrow (he maintains his imposing bulk with daily workouts), and he now owns a gold store and mortgage company in Queens, N.Y.

The notion of confronting animal abusers with a show of force is intuitively satisfying. Who doesn't want to see a bully get a taste of his own medicine? But is the threat of violence really going to change the ways of animal abusers?

Criminal justice professor Tod Burke compares Rescue Ink to the Guardian Angels, a citizen's anti-crime group that operates unarmed patrols is several cities.

"There's a fine line these guys have to be careful with, not to overstep the boundaries to become vigilantes," says Dr. Burke, a former police officer who teaches at Radford University in Virginia. As long as they stay within the boundaries of the law, he says, "I think what they're doing is beneficial."

The greatest benefit may be not in changing the behavior of the individual bad apples Rescue Ink confronts, but in the attention their show and outré image brings to the issue of animal abuse and neglect.

"If it's getting the message about animal abuse out there, to me that's the most significant thing these guys are doing," Dr. Burke says.

There is no way to know for sure what happens once the burly men and the cameras following them go away, but Rescue Ink member George, aka G, believes their presence is an effective deterrent.

"We knock on people's doors, they'll give us everything but the kitchen sink," says George, a landscaper. "They don't want to see us a second time."

And does the implied threat of violence ever slip into the real thing?

"To tell you the truth," George says, "that's what we take commercial breaks for."

• 30 •

CHANGING THE WORLD –
ONE DOG (OR CAT) AT A TIME

A new kind of underground railroad is shepherding dogs and cats rescued from U.S. shelters to safety – and new families – in Canada.

Every weekend, volunteer drivers load up their cars with furry refugees and cross the border, sometimes following the very same routes that once guided runaway slaves to freedom. Each driver handles a roughly hour-long leg, rendezvousing and transferring animals in parking lots and rest stops until they reach their destination.

One such network, Open Arms Pound Rescue, has moved an estimated 2,000 dogs (and a few cats) from shelters in the South and Midwest since it started in 2007. Co-founder Lucy Moye, based in Michigan, was working with a high-kill shelter in Ohio when she realized she could save a lot more dogs if she could match them with adoptive families and rescue groups in other areas.

Her inspiration was a little Manchester terrier called Kirby she saw at a Kentucky shelter on Petfinder.com. "He was just the picture of misery, sitting there hunched up, looking like he didn't have a friend in the world," Ms. Moye recalls. She sponsored the dog and helped find a home for it, later receiving a picture of Kirby running joyfully through a field with his new family.

"That's the paycheck," Ms. Moye said. "I can't change the world, but I can change the world for one dog."

But why Canada? Some critics argue that there are already enough homeless dogs to care for without importing them.

Cross-border rescuers understand the concern, but say the country has compassion – and rescue capacity – to spare.

"I think we are a more compassionate society. We treat our animals as basically part of our family," said Deb Wilson of Vineland, Ont., who owns an antique store and runs Ontario Weimaraner Rescue in her free time. She regularly crosses the border with van loads of homeless dogs. "Down in the South, it's sad to say, but a lot of dogs, they're disposable to people."

The American shelters the organizations work with are so overcrowded that even healthy, young, adoptable dogs have almost no chance of escaping euthanasia. And U.S. pounds can sometimes supply specific breeds that are in demand but not readily available in Canadian shelters. The rescue groups that receive the animals say they place local dogs first before re-homing ones from south of the border.

"These rescues are not turning their back on their own neighborhood dogs," Ms. Moye said.

Despite the good intentions, crossing the border isn't always smooth sailing.

A few years ago, Ms. Moye said, volunteers were frequently stopped and detained. At one point, Canadian customs officers were assessing the rescue dogs at $300 each and demanding the drivers pay taxes on them.

Ms. Wilson has since obtained a ruling from Revenue Canada specifying that rescue dogs have no monetary value; all volunteer drivers now carry a copy. And they know to have the dogs' paperwork in order, too: Health regulations require rabies certificates to be hand-signed by a veterinarian, for example.

"Two years ago it was a bit of a hassle; now it works like clockwork," Ms. Moye said.

That's thanks in large part to her massive network of animal lovers willing to spend their own time and gas money in exchange for a few tail wags.

Volunteer Brenda Bunn remembers a Chihuahua named Sophia Rose, rescued from a pound in Kentucky where she'd spent her time cowering in the corner. It turns out she was paralyzed in her hind end, the result of being shot. Her new family in Canada tricked her out with a little Chihuahua-sized wheelchair, and she recently won a doggie Paralympics-style race. "She beat a German shepherd!" Ms. Bunn said proudly.

She recalls another dog, a four-year-old cocker spaniel, whose family dropped it off at a high-kill U.S. pound on their way home from the pet store where they'd just bought a new puppy. The cocker spaniel would have been euthanized for lack of space if a volunteer had not happened to be in the lobby when it was surrendered.

"It can be the most heartbreaking thing," said Ms. Bunn, a financial planner in Peterborough, Ont., who drives dogs and runs Loyal Dog Rescue in her spare time.

The spaniel eventually found a forever home in Canada.

"When I get an e-mail three months later that tells me how amazing the dog is and how they can't imagine life without the dog, and how well the dog is living, that does it for me," Ms. Bunn said. "That keeps me going."

CANINE SEARCHERS HELP IN HAITI

When the news hit that a devastating earthquake had struck Haiti, Silvie Montier rushed to help. And so did her dog.

Three days after the quake, Ms. Montier, a founding member of the Edmonton-based Canadian Search and Disaster Dogs Association, and her Laekenois Belgian Shepherd, Cramique, boarded a plane with three other dogs and their handlers to look for survivors in the rubble.

"The earthquake itself was one of the worst I have ever seen," said Ms. Montier, who has volunteered with her dogs in disaster areas around the world (her day job is as a lawyer for a nurses' union). "Typically when there are bodies they are picked up soon after; here they were staying there on the side of the road for days. It was really very bad."

Her dog had to jump over dead bodies in some cases to search for live people. That, combined with the heat and the ever-present dust, made Haiti a tough assignment. Cramique is trained to give an alert when he finds a dead body, and to bark when he smells a live one. By the second day, Ms. Montier said, the dogs stopped alerting to cadavers; there were simply too many of them.

There were success stories, though. Ms. Montier and Cramique found a man in his 50s buried in the rubble of a collapsed house. The rest of his family had died in the earthquake, but thanks to Cramique, after four days trapped in the rubble he was saved. Ms. Montier did not get to talk to the man – once her dog smells a person, she and the dog back off and let the rescue crews with heavy equipment extricate the victim – but she did hear from many other grateful Haitians.

Over three days in Haiti helping with rescue effort, the team of four dogs found a total of six survivors.

"I found the Haitian people very good to us," Ms. Montier said. "They certainly love Canadians. I had a young man said to me, 'Oh, you're Canadian, all Canadians are my family, I will help you.' "

Ms. Montier got her first taste of search and rescue dogs' capabilities as a child growing up in war-torn Algeria, where her father was a doctor with the French army. One day, her sister wandered away on the army base where they lived, and their family dog – another Belgian Shepherd – found her at the bottom of a bomb crater. Ms. Montier was impressed, and hooked.

She soon trained the dog to find her pet turtle wherever she hid it in the yard.

Though Ms. Montier is loyal to Belgian Shepherds, she said any kind of dog can work in search and rescue. Some of the best are mutts rescued from animal shelters. There are a half-dozen search-and-rescue dog organizations in Canada, with dozens of dogs that can search for people lost in wilderness, avalanches, bomb sites and even underwater. The team Ms. Montier took to Haiti included a yellow lab, a Springer spaniel and a mixed breed.

"Any dog who loves to play ball or loves to tug" has potential, Ms. Montier said. In training, when dogs find a live person they get to play with their toy. So their barking when they find a victim in the rubble may sound like, "I found a person, come and save them!" but actually they're saying, "I found a person, give me my toy already!"

"It's a game for the dog," Ms. Montier said. It usually takes about two years to fully train a search-and-rescue dog, she said, though training is an ongoing process. Dogs and their handlers must be re-certified every one to three years. When she and Cramique returned to Canada from Haiti, they were both exhausted – all the dogs slept through the entire flight home, she said (as service dogs, they are allowed to travel in the passenger compartment). The next day, she and Cramique were doing training exercises again.

"Training is a happy game," Ms. Montier said. "Cramique loves to work. If he doesn't work he gets very bored and very destructive."

Ms. Montier said she would love to see more dogs trained for search and rescue in Canada, and more utilization of the search dogs here. In Haiti, she said, there were 175 search dogs on the ground, and her team were the only dogs from Canada.

"It's really a pity," she said. "When we arrived, we could have used an extra hundred dogs."

• 32 •

WHEN COTTONTAIL JUST
DOESN'T WANT TO RUN FREE

When it comes to infestations, bunnies are probably the cutest one you could have.

Still, 1,600 bunnies is a problem - that's how many the University of Victoria estimates are living on its campus, the latest count in a continuing feral rabbit explosion that has spanned more than two decades now. Recently, the B.C. Supreme Court ruled that the university could continue its bunny-control plan after an injunction by an animal-rights activist.

Where did all these rabbits come from? They're the progeny of abandoned pets.

Of course, you can't blame the bunnies for multiplying. That is, after all, what bunnies do best. Blame the idiot humans who caused the problem by dumping their pet bunnies on the UVic campus.

It's hard to understand the mindset of a pet dumper - seriously, they can't even take the time to drive to a no-kill shelter? But clearly, too many people view pets as disposable. And if culling the rabbit population in Victoria is a necessary short-term solution, maybe a long-term solution means enforcing some owner-control measures instead.

"We picked one up last week, a beautiful fawn-coloured bunny, plump as could be," said Laura-Leah Shaw, a bunny rescuer, local realtor and Green Party candidate. "I walked over to pick the bunny up and the bunny's like, 'OK, let me snuggle in your arms.' He couldn't have been on the ground more than 24 hours. It must be so bewildering to them. They must be wondering where their people are."

Ms. Shaw theorized that people may think they're doing their pet Cottontail a favour by letting him or her "run free." But that couldn't be further from the truth. Rabbit colonies have established hierarchies, she said, and new members sometimes have to fight their way in, not to mention the dangers posed by cars and predators.

"You're sentencing that rabbit to almost certain death," Ms. Shaw said. "It's terrible."

Ironically, while it's perfectly legal to trap and kill wild rabbits, in order to save the UVic bunnies Ms. Shaw had to jump (or rather, hop) through a number of bureaucratic hoops. Getting government permission to relocate the bunnies to the Wild Rose Rescue Ranch in East Texas took about seven weeks and 100 pages of documentation, Ms. Shaw said. Why Texas? She started calling locally and fanned out - the Texas refuge was the first place she found willing to take in more than a thousand bunnies.

How about a more permanent solution to the bunny-dumping problem, one that doesn't rely on the kindness of Texas strangers? That might require some political will. The city of Richmond has banned the sale of pet-store bunnies; Kelowna and North Vancouver require that any rabbits sold at pet stores be spayed and neutered. Activists would like to see the spay-neuter law go province-wide, if not national; they also think hefty fines for animal dumping would be a good deterrent.

Actually, if you really want to deter these people, I have a few ideas. Some humble suggestions on appropriate punishments for dumping pets:

- Drive the former pet owners to the middle of the Yukon and then kick them out of the car, without food or water. "Where's Daddy?" "Oh, he went to a nice farm where he can run and play with all his friends..."

- Mandatory spay and neuter - of irresponsible owners

- We tell your kids what you really did to the family pet, with photos of what happened when Topsy met Mr. Coyote.

- Relocation to East Texas - again, for the owners.

"You see this cruelty to bunnies all over the country," said Joseph Martinez, one of several vets who is spaying and neutering the UVic bunnies before their Texas trip. Dr. Martinez feels a special kinship with rabbits. He grew up poor in Israel's Negev Desert, the son of Italian immigrants who eked out a living farming and raising rabbits for meat.

"Those bunnies really saved our lives," said Dr. Martinez, who became a vegetarian before pursuing a career in animal medicine. "There's a spiritual connection between me and bunnies."

You don't need to have a spiritual connection to know that dumping your pet is wrong - common decency will suffice. Unfortunately, decency towards animals is sometimes anything but common. These Texas-bound bunnies are lucky - even if they'll have to learn to hop wearing 10-gallon hats.

SHELTER CONNECTS FAITH
WITH FURRY FRIENDS

Robin Nafshi has always loved animals. And she's always loved Judaism. But until recently, the Reform rabbi thought that never the twain shall meet.

All that's changed, though, as Ms. Nafshi, president of a new kind of animal sanctuary in New Jersey, is creating avenues for animal-loving Jews to connect their faith with their furry friends.

"We are a very human-centered religion, and most Jews who are passionate about animal kindness don't find they have a voice within their religious tradition," Ms. Nafshi said, "which is unfortunate, because it's such a deep part of our tradition. From the very beginning of our creation story, we are the caregivers."

Ms. Nafshi serves as president of Seer Farms, which bills itself as a "people-centered animal sanctuary." The shelter opened in January 2009 to take care of pets for owners who are temporarily unable to keep them, whether due to foreclosure, illness, domestic violence, overseas deployment, eviction or other circumstances. Some animals ultimately are surrendered and get adopted, but most are reunited with their owners after the crisis has passed. Seer Farms asks for $50 a month from the owners, but doesn't turn anyone away because of inability to pay. (Regular pet-boarding services can cost upward of $50 per day.)

Located in Jackson, N.J., the sanctuary is filled to capacity with 20 dogs, about 90 cats and one rabbit. Laura Pople, a Red Cross disaster volunteer who set up a temporary shelter for animals in Lufkin, Texas, following Hurricane Katrina, is founder and executive director.

Ms. Nafshi has seen up close the ripple effect of the economic pressures that are forcing people out of their homes, pets in tow. Some of the pets' owners are living in their cars following foreclosure; others are bunking with friends or living in shelters that don't allow animals. People usually have to be pretty desperate before they give up their pets, Ms. Nafshi has found.

"We hear it all, believe me. Your heart just breaks for people," Ms. Nafshi said.

Pastoral counseling is part of Ms. Nafshi's mission as a rabbi, and she said that her involvement with Seer Farms has given her the opportunity she thought she'd never have: to combine her rabbinic role with her animal-welfare work. Ms. Nafshi serves as the associate rabbi of Temple Beth-El in Hillsborough, N.J., and as community chaplain of Ohr Tikvah Jewish Healing Center.

Her training and experience as a rabbi helps Ms. Nafshi deal with the crushing tales of woe that accompany many of the animals to the shelter. One woman asked for temporary care of her Shih Tzus while she relocated to nurse her dying mother-in-law; while she was gone, her own husband died suddenly.

Ms. Nafshi spent a recent morning at the farm walking and cuddling the dogs. "They just want to be in your lap and be loved," she said.

"I've never been here at an intake when the owners were not crying," she said. "And that includes the 22-year-old tattooed guy with the huge pit bull. Many of these people have never been apart from their animals. How do you explain to the animal that your daddy is coming back?"

In addition to using her rabbinic experience at the animal sanctuary, Ms. Nafshi brought her animal-welfare work to her congregation. Temple Beth-El held an animal-awareness week in October. Activities throughout the week included animal-themed Hebrew lessons, a dog and cat food donation drive, and a Sabbath sermon on the theme of kindness to animals.

In the spring of 2009, she hosted a blessing of the animals around Passover — a time that seemed logical to thank the sacrificial Passover lamb as well as other animals. Blessing animals is a common Christian ritual, in the tradition of St. Francis of Assisi. It's a new thing for Jews, at least in New Jersey, and people came from all over the state to have their animals blessed by Ms. Nafshi.

"It shows there's that much of a hunger for it," she said.

Ms. Nafshi, however, said she sees little widespread interest in incorporating animals and their welfare into Jewish practice. She noted that the Conservative movement has shone a spotlight on animal treatment through the Hekhsher Tzedek initiative, aimed at improving the ethics of kosher food production. But within the Reform movement, she said, "there's no momentum" for discussing animal issues.

It's an attitude Ms. Nafshi hopes to change, little by little. As Seer Farms' motto indicates, she believes that caring for animals can go hand in hand with caring for people, in both the secular and the Jewish world.

"Our hearts and our souls are big enough to embrace multiple species," Ms. Nafshi said. "It's not either-or; there's room for both, and that's very much part of our tradition."

• 34 •

THERAPY DOG BRINGS LOVE
TO KIDS IN JAIL

The girl in the beige jumpsuit shuffled into the bare room, her face lighting up when she saw the huge brown dog thumping his tail against the cold linoleum floor.

Gentle Ben, a 165-pound Newfoundland, planted a slobbery kiss on 17-year-old Alex, who's in jail for violating her parole.

When Alex first visited Ben a few days earlier, she spent most of the hour sobbing into his soft fur, her body and mind wracked by methamphetamine withdrawal.

This time, she chatted happily with Pat Dowell, Ben's handler, about her plans to kick meth, move to California with her mom, and go to college.

"I shouldn't be here," Alex said as she scratched behind Ben's ears. "I'm not like the other kids who keep coming back here. I'm not. I'm going to get out and get better."

Pat nodded approvingly, even though she's heard this before from kids who seem to cycle helplessly through the system. A former cop, Pat's not so naive to believe an hour petting her "therapy dog" will solve a kid's problems.

And yet, she has watched Ben transform hardened, violent inmates into playful little kids. She knows her big, sweet dog somehow drools his way into tough teenagers' hearts.

"The dog is a nonjudgmental, live object that gives unconditional love," Ms. Dowell said. "To walk into a room and see this mammoth animal that just wants to wag its tail and say, 'You're the most important thing in the world to me!' - it's giving that kind of emotional support they've probably never had."

Ben thrives on the attention, and the occasional doggie treat. Now the 7-year-old Newfie is getting national attention, as one of six dogs nominated for the Pedigree "Paws to Recognize" award for service dogs. Other contenders are a seeing-eye dog from California, a guard dog adopted by a Special Forces unit in Iraq, a search-and-rescue dog from Louisiana, a police dog from North Carolina, and a customs dog from Florida. People can vote online for their favorite.

Ben and Ms. Dowell visit the Clark County Juvenile Justice Center in Vancouver once a week. Ms. Dowell lets the inmates set the pace. They can talk if they want, or they can simply sit with Ben and pet him.

Ms. Dowell also teaches kids how to make Ben follow commands by using positive reinforcement and a soft voice - techniques unfamiliar to many of the children she meets.

Ben's charms have even won over corrections officers, who tend to be skeptical of this touchy-feely stuff.

"Seeing the pet therapy dog just kind of soothes kids," said Mike Riggan, manager of the 80-bed juvenile jail in southwest Washington. "Dogs love you unconditionally. It seems to ease their fears."

Ben also works at schools, a hospital, and children's camps. At the hospital, Ben helps dog-bite victims conquer their fears. They start out petting Ben's ample rear, a safe distance from his slobbery mouth, then work their way up toward the dog's head as they get more comfortable. Ben's mellow personality suits the task, Ms. Dowell said: "He's not going to make any sudden movements, believe me."

Ben's training as a therapy dog taught him how to keep calm during stressful situations, ranging from loud noises to aggressive hugs. Ms. Dowell, 48, learned to recognize signs of anxiety or fatigue in her dog. Every two years, Ben retakes a canine good citizen test to keep his status as a therapy dog.

Alex, who asked that her last name not be used, said her time with Ben raises her spirits. After an arrest for marijuana possession last fall, she's been booked into jail five times, usually for running away from wherever her probation tells her to be. She spent her 17th birthday, Thanksgiving and Christmas in jail.

Ben reminds Alex of her own dog, a devoted mutt named Homey who died several years ago. When she gets out she wants to reunite with one of Homey's relatives, a puppy named Spike.

Alex poured out her hopes and dreams as she petted Ben. She wants to move to California and hang out at the beach. She wants to get her GED and become a photojournalist. She wants someone to bring her candy this weekend. Mostly, she wants to be a better role model for her 10-year-old sister.

"I talked to her last night on the phone and I started crying," Alex said. "I was like, 'I'm sorry, I'm sorry.'"

Then she got quiet and sank down to rest her head on Ben's thick brown fur. The jail bustled with activity all around them. But for a moment everything was still in the small room, except for the sound of Ben's sleepy wheeze and the steady twitch of Alex's hand, scratching the head of a very good dog.

PUBLICATION NOTES

How my dog taught me to be a mom
Originally published May 17, 2010, in The Globe and Mail

I dress up my dog for Halloween
Originally published Oct. 16, 2009, in The Globe and Mail

My mysterious mutt: Lab, beagle or dingo?
Originally published May 6, 2008, in The Globe and Mail

Paris just isn't Paris without your pooch
Originally published June 22, 2009, in The Globe and Mail

When furbabies meet the real thing
Originally published Aug. 31, 2009, in The Globe and Mail

Dog crazy, or just plain crazy?
Originally published Aug. 26, 2008, in The Globe and Mail

Move over, Ace Ventura: Pet detectives are real
Originally published July 29, 2008, in The Globe and Mail

Is your pet Rapture-ready?
Originally published Jan. 4, 2010, in The Globe and Mail

Officer's bark is a howl, but suspects don't laugh
Originally published Sept. 25, 1997, in The Charlotte Observer

Cats v. dogs: Can't they just get along?
Originally published Oct. 7, 2008, in The Globe and Mail

How domestication has dumbed down our dogs
Originally published Sept. 5, 2010, in The Globe and Mail

Vegan pets: Where's the beef?
Originally published May 12, 2009, in The Globe and Mail

DIY pet rescue: How CPR could save your pooch
Originally published March 1, 2010, in The Globe and Mail

Cute, yummy or gross: Our (il)logic about animals
Originally published Oct. 21, 2010, in The Globe and Mail

Are the dog whisperer's method's safe?
Originally published July 12, 2010, in The Globe and Mail

The new legal hot topic: Can your pet sue?
Originally published July 15, 2008, in The Globe and Mail

There are still children starving in Africa,
but I'll still spoil my dog
Originally published Nov. 11, 2010, in The Globe and Mail

Men who love cats
Originally published March 24, 2009, in The Globe and Mail

Dog stylists unleash pets' fabulousness
Originally published June 25, 2010, on MSNBC.com

You know what your cat really needs? A pom-pom tail
Originally published Aug. 9, 2010, in The Globe and Mail

In doggy heaven, no humans allowed
Originally published July 26, 2010, in The Globe and Mail

Pupperware parties – they are the cat's meow
Originally published June 9, 2009, in The Globe and Mail

Is your pet ... psychic?
Originally published May 18, 2009, in The Globe and Mail

Lady Gaga, doggie-style
Originally published April 12, 2010, in The Globe and Mail

These pets have more Facebook friends than you

HEAVY PETTING

Originally published Aug. 23, 2010, in The Globe and Mail

Psycho kitty, qu'est-ce que c'est?
Originally published July 6, 2009, in The Globe and Mail

New dog science could also help humans
Originally published Oct. 12, 2009, in The Globe and Mail

Soldiers help canine refugees
Originally published May 3, 2010, in The Globe and Mail

Tough guys, tender hearts
Originally published Jan. 18, 2010, in The Globe and Mail

Changing the world – one dog (or cat) at a time
Originally published June 14, 2010, in The Globe and Mail

Canine searchers help in Haiti
Originally published Feb. 1, 2010, in The Globe and Mail

When cottontail just doesn't want to run free
Originally published Sept. 20, 2010, in The Globe and Mail

Shelter connects faith with furry friends
Originally published Nov. 4, 2009, in The Forward

Therapy dog brings love to kids in jail
Originally published May 2, 2004, by The Associated Press

ABOUT THE AUTHOR

Rebecca Dube is a sucker for a wet nose and a wagging tail.

As Canada's premier pet columnist, she wrote the "Heavy Petting" column about pets and the people who love them for The Globe and Mail, Canada's national newspaper.

Her love of pets began with a roly-poly black Lab puppy named Star, whose love and devotion was matched only by her affection for tennis balls. Rebecca discovered a love of books while making her way through the C.S. Lewis Narnia series, and as a child, she spent many happy hours in the company of both dog and books.

Rebecca has worked as a journalist for The Associated Press, USA Today, The Charlotte Observer, The Globe and Mail, The Forward, The Christian Science Monitor and TODAY.com, and somehow has managed to sneak in animal stories everywhere she goes.

Rebecca grew up in Baltimore and graduated from Yale University. She lives in New York City with her husband, who is also a journalist, and her young son, who is also very curious.

ACKNOWLEDGEMENTS

Rebecca would like to thank Star, Polly, Lucky, Mama Cat, Butch, Rascal, Bridgette, Ranger, Merlin and Lily. She would also like to thank her parents, for keeping so many pets, and for always encouraging her to follow her dreams. Thanks, finally, to her husband Jon, for making this happen and for making everything more fun.